STEEL BUILDING DESIGN: CONCISE EUROCODES

REVISED EDITION

SCI PUBLICATION P362

STEEL BUILDING DESIGN: CONCISE EUROCODES

In accordance with Eurocodes and the UK National Annexes

Brettle, M.E. BEng

Brown, D.G. BEng CEng MICE

Revised edition:

Georgakis, M. MEng, MSc, DIC

Couchman, G.H. MA, PhD, CEng, MICE

SCI
Steel Knowledge

SCI (The Steel Construction Institute) is the leading, independent provider of technical expertise and disseminator of best practice to the steel construction sector. We work in partnership with clients, members and industry peers to help build businesses and provide competitive advantage through the commercial application of our knowledge. We are committed to offering and promoting sustainable and environmentally responsible solutions.

Our service spans the following areas:

Membership
Individual & corporate membership

Advice
Members advisory service

Information
Publications
Education
Events & training

Consultancy
Development
Product development
Engineering support
Sustainability

Assessment
SCI Assessment

Specification
Websites
Engineering software

Publication Number: **SCI P362**

ISBN 13: 978-1-85942-236-6

Published by:
SCI, Silwood Park, Ascot,
Berkshire. SL5 7QN UK

T: +44 (0)1344 636525
F: +44 (0)1344 636570
E: reception@steel-sci.com

www.steel-sci.com

To report any errors, contact:
publications@steel-sci.com

British Library Cataloguing-in-Publication Data.
A catalogue record for this book is available from the British Library.

The text paper in this publication is totally chlorine free. The paper manufacturer and the printers have been independently certified in accordance with the rules of the Forest Stewardship Council.

FSC www.fsc.org MIX Paper from responsible sources FSC® C020438

recycle
When you have finished with this please recycle it.

FOREWORD

Since the withdrawal in March 2010 of earlier British Standards, the design of steel framed buildings in the UK, including those where composite (steel and concrete) construction is used, has increasingly been carried out in accordance with the Eurocodes.

For steel framed buildings, the main Eurocode Part that needs to be consulted is BS EN 1993-1-1 and its National Annex. Reference is also needed to BS EN 1990 and BS EN 1991-1-1, together with their National Annexes, in order to determine the design values of the effects of actions.

Those Eurocode documents are comprehensive, covering more situations than normally found within the scope of ordinary multi-storey buildings. To help the designer, this guide selects those rules most commonly needed for the design of orthodox multi storey buildings and presents them in a single concise document. Particular items of non-contradictory complementary information (NCCI) that would be of assistance are included alongside the selected Eurocode clauses.

This publication provides the key requirements from BS EN 1990, BS EN 1991-1-1 and certain parts of BS EN 1993 (mainly from Part 1-1 but also from Parts 1-5, 1-8 and 1-10). Since steel framed buildings often have composite floor beams, brief references are made to BS EN 1994-1-1 and to BS EN 1992-1-1.

NCCI information is distinguished from the requirements derived from the Eurocode Parts and their National Annexes by a dark blue shading behind the text, tables and graphics.

This publication was prepared by Mary Brettle and David Brown, with assistance from James Way and David Iles, all of SCI. A reprint in November 2011 included a number of corrections to minor typographical mistakes that were present in the first print run of November 2009.

The document was revised in 2017 to reflect the latest thinking on the Eurocodes and lessons learned during their application. It also recognises that S355 is now the default steel grade in the UK, with a growing use of S460. This revision was prepared by Michail Georgakis and Graham Couchman, both of SCI.

The preparation of the revised edition was funded by SCI and ArcelorMittal Europe.

CONTENTS

SUMMARY

This publication provides a concise compilation of selected rules in the Eurocodes, together with relevant non-contradictory complementary information, that relate to the design of common forms of steel building structure in the UK. The basis of structural design is briefly reviewed and guidance is given on the principal actions and combinations of actions that need to be considered in orthodox building structures. Rules from BS EN 1993-1-1 for global analysis, bending and axial resistance are presented. In a significant change for this revised edition, requirements for toughness against brittle fracture in 'quasi-static' structures are given (rather than the requirements of PD 6696-1-10, that now only need be applied to structures subject to fatigue). Design rules for simple bolted and welded connections, from BS EN 1993-1-8 are presented. The outline rules for composite construction are summarized; it is assumed that software will be used for the design of composite beams and composite slabs. The appendices include guidance on selection of the most critical combination of actions, simplified expressions for interaction factors for combined bending and axial force, and a simplified approach for lateral torsional buckling resistance of unrestrained lengths of beams.

Since the original of this publication was produced in 2009, SCI has published a number of volumes of worked examples. Experience from SCI's Technical Advisory Service suggests that readers may find these useful in gaining a better understanding of some of the concepts contained in the present publication.

INTRODUCTION

1.1 Scope

1. This publication provides a concise compilation of the principles and application rules in the Eurocodes that relate to the design of common forms of building structure in the UK. Designs in accordance with this guide will automatically conform with the Eurocodes, as implemented by the UK National Annexes, to the extent covered by the scope defined in (4).
2. This guide covers parts of BS EN 1990, *Eurocode: Basis of Structural Design*, BS EN 1991, *Eurocode 1: Actions on Structures*, and *BS EN 1993, Eurocode 3: Design of steel structures*. Small sections of BS EN 1994, *Eurocode 4: Design of Composite steel and concrete structures* and BS EN 1992 *Eurocode 2: Design of concrete structures* are included, for reference when designing buildings with composite floors.
3. A general introduction to the Eurocodes, which describes the format, lists the many separate Eurocode Parts that relate to the full range of steel and composite structures and introduces the role of the National Annexes, is given in SCI publication P361 *Steel building design: Introduction to the Eurocodes*.
4. This guide covers the design of orthodox members in steel frames. It does not cover portal frames, stainless steel, and cold-formed sections. Certain practical limitations are given to the scope – for example to exclude the rules that cover the design of Class 4 sections. This guide does not address the fire design of structures, torsion, or fatigue.
5. Guidance on topics excluded from the scope of this publication and on more detailed evaluation of some aspects may be found in the following SCI publications:

   Joints in Steel Construction – Simple connections in accordance with BS EN 1993-1-1 (P358)
   Joints in Steel Construction – Moment-resisting joints to Eurocode 3 (P398)
   Composite design of steel framed buildings (P359)
   Design of composite beams with large web openings (P355)
   Stability of steel beams and columns (P360)
   Steel building design: Design data (P363)
   Steel building design: Design data - Universal Column resistances in S460M steel (P404)
   Steel building design: Worked examples – Open sections (P364)
   Steel building design: Medium rise braced frames (P365)

Steel building design: Worked examples – Hollow sections (P374)
Fire resistance design of steel framed buildings (P375)
Resistance of beams and columns in fire – Worked examples to the Eurocodes (P403)
Design of steel beams in torsion (P385)
Structural robustness of steel framed buildings (P391)
Brittle fracture: Selection of steel sub-grade to BS EN 1993-1-10 (P419).

1.2 Format

BS EN 1990, 1.4

1. All the clauses and paragraphs in this guide are numbered consecutively. Reference to the Eurocode clauses from which the guidance is derived are given in the left-hand margin of each page.
2. In the Eurocodes, a distinction is made between Principles and Application Rules. Principles are identified by the letter P following the paragraph number. Application Rules are generally recognised rules which comply with the Principles and satisfy their requirements. This distinction has been preserved in this book.

> Non-contradictory complementary information (NCCI) is given in shaded boxes, as for this text. Three types of NCCI are included:
> - Clarification of Eurocode rules
> - General design guidance (such as UK preferences for products or details)
> - Additional application rules, taken from other published sources
>
> (Note that there is no definition in the Eurocodes of what constitutes NCCI; it is merely another source of information that complements the Eurocodes but does not contradict them.)

3. In Appendix A, the rules relating to the procedures for verifying common types of steel members are summarised as a series of design steps. Appendix A covers:
   - Simply supported beams
   - Tension members
   - Compression members
   - Compression members with moments
   - Columns in simple construction

1.3 Definitions

1. Special terms are defined where they first appear in each clause. The Eurocode terminology is generally particular and precise, with the intention of providing clarity and avoiding ambiguity.

1.4 Symbols

1. Symbols are generally defined where they are used within the text.
2. The Eurocode system for symbols generally adopts a common notation for the principal variables. Differentiation between related variables, such as axial force and

compression resistance, is achieved by the use of subscripts. Multiple subscripts are used where necessary, for example to distinguish between design bending resistance about the y-y and z-z axes; each component is separated by a comma.

3. A list of the most common symbols used is given in Appendix B.
4. In this guide, a dot is used as the decimal separator, in line with existing UK practice. The Eurocodes themselves use a comma as the separator.

1.5 Terminology

The Eurocodes contain a number of terms that will be unfamiliar to designers experienced in the use of earlier British Standards. Some important differences are given below.

Table 1.1 Eurocode terminology

Eurocode term	Equivalent
Actions	Loads
Permanent action	Dead load
Variable action	Imposed, or live load
Design value of actions	Ultimate loads
Verification	Check
Effects	Internal bending moments and forces which result from the application of the actions
Resistance	Capacity, or Resistance
Effects of deformed geometry	Second-order effects

BASIS OF STRUCTURAL DESIGN

This Section includes the key principles and application rules in BS EN 1990 that relate to the design of steel structures and some general requirements extracted from BS EN 1993-1-1, BS EN 1993-1-5 and BS EN 1993-1-8. For a full presentation of the basis of structural design, the use of design by the partial factor method to achieve required levels of reliability, consult BS EN 1990 and the commentary by Gulvanessian et al[1].

2.1 General requirements

References given in margin for Sections 2.1 to 2.3 are to BS EN 1990 and its National Annex.

2.1.1 Basic requirements

2.1(1)P

1.(P) A structure shall be designed and executed (constructed) in such a way that it will:

- Sustain all actions likely to occur
- Remain fit for use during its intended life
- Have adequate structural resistance, serviceability and durability.
- Not be damaged by events such as explosions to an extent that is disproportionate to the cause.

Note: Clause 2.1 of EN 1990 should be consulted for the complete list of basic requirements relating to structural design to the Eurocodes.

2.1(6)

2. The basic requirements given in (1) should be satisfied by the use of appropriate materials, design and detailing, and quality control.

2.1(5)P

3.(P) Potential damage shall be avoided or limited by appropriate choice of one or more of the following:

- Avoiding, eliminating or reducing the hazards to which the structure can be subjected
- Selecting a structural form which has low sensitivity to the hazards considered
- Selecting a structural form and design that can survive adequately the accidental removal of an individual member or a limited part of the structure, or the occurrence of acceptable localised damage
- Avoiding as far as possible structural systems that can collapse without warning
- Tying the structural members together.

[1] *Designers' Guide to EN 1990*, Second edition, ICE Publishing, 2012.

2.1.2 Reliability

1.(P) The reliability required for structures within the scope of this guide shall be achieved by:
- Design in accordance with this guide
- Appropriate execution and quality management measures

2.2(4) 2. The reliability that is required for a structure may be specified by the classification of the whole structure and/or classification of its individual components.

2.2(3) 3. The required level of reliability for a structure should be selected by considering relevant factors, including:
- Possible cause and/or mode of attaining a limit state
- Possible consequences of failure, e.g. loss of life, economical loss.
- Public aversion to failure of the structure
- Expense and procedures required to reduce the risk of failure.

2.1.3 Design working life

2.3(1) 1. Buildings other than agricultural, temporary and monumental buildings should be designed for a working life of 50 years.

> 50 years is the normal design working life for buildings in the UK, and this is reflected in the characteristic values of actions found in Eurocode 1 and the partial factors applied to those actions. It is possible to vary the design values of actions to reflect a longer or shorter working life, but this is beyond the scope of this publication. The length of working life affects the design values of the effects of actions, but not the resistance and serviceability verifications presented in this publication

2.2 Design situations

3.2(2)P 1.(P) Design situations shall be classified as:

Persistent	normal conditions of use
Transient	temporary conditions applicable to the structure e.g. loads applied during execution
Accidental	exceptional conditions applicable to the structure or to its exposure e.g. fire, explosion or the consequence of localised failure.
Seismic	conditions that are applicable to the structure during a seismic event.

> The most common design situation is the Persistent situation. The Accidental situation covers situations such as exceptional drifted snow and robustness requirements. Design situations during construction or refurbishment are transient situations. Seismic design is outside the scope of this guide.

6.3.1(1)

2.3 Verification by the partial factor method

2.3.1 Design values

1. The design value of an action (F_d) can be expressed as:

$$F_d = \gamma_F \psi F_k$$

where:

γ_F is the partial factor for the action (expressed as γ_G for permanent actions, γ_Q, for variable actions)

ψ is the combination factor and is equal to 1.0 for permanent actions and ψ_0; ψ_1; or ψ_2 for variable actions. The ψ factor for variable actions depends on the combination of actions being considered, see Table 2.2.

F_k is the characteristic value of the action.

> The design value of an action is not usually expressed as a value in its own right; BS EN 1990 usually refers to the product $\gamma_F \psi F_k$ (or simply $\gamma_F F_k$). Permanent and variable actions are distinguished symbolically by the use of G_k for permanent actions and Q_k for variable actions.

2. The design value of a material property can be expressed as:

$$F_d = \frac{X_k}{\gamma_M}$$

where:

X_k is a characteristic value of the material

γ_M is the partial factor for a material property

> The design value of a material property is not often expressed as a value in its own right.

3. The design value of resistance can be expressed as a function of the design value of the material property and geometrical data:

$$R_d = \left\{ \frac{X_k}{\gamma_M} ; a \right\}$$

where:

a is the geometric parameter.

> Thus, for the design resistance of a cross section, $N_{c,Rd} = \dfrac{Af_y}{\gamma_{M0}}$, see 6.2.4.
>
> In this case the geometrical parameter is the area, A.

2.3.2 Ultimate limit states

6.4.1(1)P

1.(P) The following ultimate limit states shall be verified:

EQU Loss of static equilibrium of the structure or any part of it considered as a rigid body, where, minor variations in the value or the spatial distribution of actions from a single source are significant, and the strengths of construction materials or ground are generally not governing.

STR Failure or excessive deformation of the structure or structural member including footings, piles and basement walls, etc. where the strength of the structural material governs.

> The STR limit state is normally the only limit state that needs to be considered.
>
> The EQU limit state only rarely needs to be verified (it might be necessary for a light structure subject to wind load that is not fixed against uplift, and so susceptible to overturning, or is not restrained against sliding).
>
> BS EN 1990 also requires verification of two further limit states:
>
> GEO Failure or excessive deformation of the ground where the strength of the soil or rock are significant in providing resistance.
>
> FAT Fatigue failure of the structure or structural members.
>
> The design of foundations and fatigue design are both outside the scope of this guide.

6.4.2(3)P

2.(P) When considering a limit state of rupture or excessive deformation of a section, member or connection (STR) it shall be verified that:

$$E_d \le R_d$$

where:

E_d is the design value of the effect of actions such as internal force, moment or a vector representing several internal forces or moments

R_d is the design value of the corresponding resistance.

2.3.3 Combination of actions at ULS

2.3.3.1 General

6.4.3.1(1)P

1. For each design situation, the design values of the effects of the action(s) should be determined from the combination of the actions that may occur simultaneously.

6.4.3.1(2)

2. Each combination of actions should include a leading or main variable action, or an accidental action.

6.4.3.1(6)

3. Imposed deformations should be taken into account, where relevant.

2.3.3.2 Persistent or transient design situations

6.4.3.2(2)

1. The combination of effects of actions to be considered should be based on:
   - the design value of the permanent actions
   - the design value of the leading variable action
   - the design combination values of the accompanying variable actions.

2. The combinations of actions may either be expressed as:

6.10

$$\sum_{j\geq 1}\gamma_{G,j}G_{k,j}\text{ "+" }\gamma_{Q,1}Q_{k,1}\text{ "+" }\sum_{i>1}\gamma_{Q,i}\psi_{0,i}Q_{k,i}$$

or alternatively, for the STR limit state, the less favourable of the two following expressions:

6.10a

$$\sum_{j\geq 1}\gamma_{G,j}G_{k,j}\text{ "+" }\gamma_{Q,1}\psi_{0,1}Q_{k,1}\text{ "+" }\sum_{i>1}\gamma_{Q,i}\psi_{0,i}Q_{k,i}$$

6.10b

$$\sum_{j\geq 1}\xi_j\gamma_{G,j}G_{k,j}\text{ "+" }\gamma_{Q,1}Q_{k,1}\text{ "+" }\sum_{i>1}\gamma_{Q,i}\psi_{0,i}Q_{k,i}$$

where:

"+" implies "to be combined with"

Σ implies "the combined effect of"

$G_{k,j}$ are the characteristic values of the permanent actions

$Q_{k,1}$ is the characteristic value of one of the variable actions

$Q_{k,i}$ are the characteristic values of the other variable actions

$\gamma_{G,j}$ is the partial factor for the permanent action $G_{k,j}$ (see (3))

$\gamma_{Q,i}$ is the partial factor for the variable action Q_{ki} (see (3))

$\psi_{0,i}$ is the ψ_0 factor for the combination value of the variable action Q_{ki} (see Table 2.2)

NA.2.2.3.2

ξ is a reduction factor applied to unfavourable permanent actions (in 6.10b) $= 0.925$

Although Note 1 of EN 1990 A1.2.1(1) states that 'depending on its uses and the form and the location of a building, the combinations of actions may be based on not more than two variable actions', NA 2.2.1 states that 'all effects of actions that can exist simultaneously should be considered together in combination of actions'.

Expression (6.10) gives slightly conservative results when compared to expressions (6.10a) and (6.10b), which are therefore recommended given they are only marginally more complicated.

Expression (6.10b) will normally be the governing case in the UK.

Note that (6.10a) and (6.10b) can only be used for the STR and GEO limit states.

3. The partial factors to be used in the combination of actions are given in Table 2.1 and the factors on accompanying actions are given in Table 2.2.

Tables NA.A1.2(A) and NA.A1.2(B)

Table 2.1 Partial factor for actions (γ_F)

Ultimate Limit State	Permanent Actions $\gamma_{G,i}$		Leading or Main Variable Action	Accompanying Variable Action
	Unfavourable	Favourable	$\gamma_{Q,1}$	$\gamma_{Q,1}$
EQU	1.1	0.9	1.5	1.5
STR	1.35	1.0	1.5	1.5

Note: When variable actions are favourable, that is they relieve the effect being considered, Q_k should be taken as zero

Table NA.A1.1

Table 2.2 Values of ψ factors for buildings

Action	ψ_0	ψ_1	ψ_2
Imposed loads in buildings, category (see EN 1991-1-1)			0.3
Category A: domestic, residential areas	0.7	0.5	0.3
Category B: office areas	0.7	0.5	0.3
Category C: congregation areas	0.7	0.7	0.6
Category D: shopping areas	0.7	0.7	0.6
Category E: storage areas	1.0	0.9	0.8
Category H: roofs*	0.7	0	0
Snow loads on buildings (see EN 1991-3)			
- for sites located at altitude $H > 1\ 000$ m a.s.l.	0.70	0.50	0.20
- for sites located at altitude $H \leq 1\ 000$ m a.s.l.	0.50	0.20	0
Wind loads on buildings (see (EN 1991-1-4)	0.5	0.2	0
Temperature (non-fire) in buildings (see EN 1991-1-5)	0.6	0.5	0

BS EN 1991-1-1 3.3.2(1)

**** On roofs, imposed loads should not be combined with either wind loads or snow loads - see 3.1(4).***

2.3.3.3 Accidental design situations

1. The combination of actions for accidental design situations can be expressed as:

Eq (6.11b) and Table NA.A1.3

$$\sum_{j\geq 1} G_{k,j} \text{"+"} A_d \text{"+"} \psi_{1,1} Q_{k,1} \text{"+"} \sum_{i>1} \psi_{2,i} Q_{k,i}$$

where:

A_d is the design value of an accidental action

$\psi_{1,1}$ is the ψ_1 factor for the frequent value of the variable action $Q_{k,i}$ (see Table 2.2)

$\psi_{2,i}$ is the ψ_2 factor for the quasi-permanent value of the variable action $Q_{k,i}$ (see Table 2.2)

The accidental combination of actions is used when verifying the tying resistance of a structure. In England and Wales Approved Document A of the Building Regulations gives the requirements for reducing the sensitivity of the building to disproportionate collapse. Similar requirements are given in *Technical Handbook Domestic* for Scotland and in *Technical Booklet D – Structure* for Northern Ireland.

2.3.4 Serviceability limit states

6.5.1(1)

2.(P) It shall be verified that:

$$E_d \leq C_d$$

where:

E_d is the design value of the effect of actions specified in the serviceability criterion, determined on the basis of the relevant combination

C_d is the limiting design value of the relevant combination.

> For the serviceability limit state, the partial factors for actions (γ_F) are implicitly taken as 1.0 and are therefore not shown in the expressions for the effects of actions.

2.3.5 Combination of actions for SLS

1. The combinations of actions for serviceability limit states are:

Characteristic	used for irreversible limit states.
Frequent	used for reversible limit states.
Quasi-permanent	used for long-term effects and the appearance of the structure.

2. The expressions for the effects due to the combinations of actions are:

Characteristic combination

(6.14b)

$$\sum_{j\geq1} G_{k,j} \text{"+"} Q_{k,1} \text{"+"} \sum_{i>1} \psi_{0,i} Q_{k,i}$$

Frequent combination

(6.15b)

$$\sum_{j\geq1} G_{k,j} \text{"+"} \psi_{1,i} Q_{k,1} \text{"+"} \sum_{i>1} \psi_{2,i} Q_{k,i}$$

Quasi-permanent combination

(6.16b)

$$\sum_{j\geq1} G_{k,j} \text{"+"} \sum_{i\geq1} \psi_{2,i} Q_{k,i}$$

where:

$\psi_{1,1}$ is the ψ factor for the frequent value of the variable action Q_{ki} (see Table 2.2)

$\psi_{2,i}$ is the ψ factor for the quasi-permanent value of the variable action Q_{ki} (see Table 2.2).

> Advice on which combination to use is given in the Eurocode for the relevant material (BS EN 1993-1-1 for steel buildings) and its National Annex. The National Annex to BS EN 1993-1-1 states that serviceability deflections should be based on the unfactored variable actions, and that permanent actions should not be included. See Section 7 of this publication.

2.4 General requirements for steel structures

References given in margin for Section 2.4 are to BS EN 1993-1-1 and its National Annex.

2.4.1 Basic requirements

Based on 2.1.1(1) P

1.(P) The design of steel structures within the scope of this guide shall be in accordance with the general rules in Section 2.1.

Based on 2.1.1(4)

2. The rules for resistances, serviceability and durability given in this guide should be applied.

2.4.2 Reliability management

1. The level of reliability should be achieved by the use of appropriate quality management in design and execution.

2.1.2(1)

2. Execution class should be in accordance with BS EN 1993-1-1 Annex C. Execution class EXC2 should normally be specified for buildings.

> BS EN 1993-1-1 Annex C considers four classes of requirements for execution (construction) of the structure as a whole, or of components of a structure, denoted EXC1 to EXC4. Strictness requirements increase from EXC1 to EXC4. The choice is a function of the Reliability and/or Consequences Class (concepts described in BS EN 1990) and loading. For buildings within the scope of this guide, EXC2 will normally be sufficient, indeed BS EN 1990-2 states this should be the default if no class is specified, and the UK National Structural Steelwork Specification (NSSS) presumes EXC2.

2.4.3 Design working life

2.1.3.2(3)B
2.1.3.3(3)B

1. For structural components that cannot be designed for the total design life of the building, (see 2.1.3), their safe removal and replacement should be verified as a transient design situation.

2.4.4 Durability

2.1.3.3(2)B

1. The effects of deterioration of steel due to corrosion should be accounted for by the appropriate selection of material, or by structural redundancy and by the use of appropriate corrosion protection.
2. Protective coatings should be applied to structural members in accordance with BS EN 1090.

4(6)B

3. For buildings where the internal relative humidity does not exceed 80%, corrosion protection does not need to be applied to internal steelwork.

4(2), 4(3)

4. Parts susceptible to corrosion or mechanical wear should be designed such that inspection, maintenance and reconstruction can be carried out satisfactorily and access is available for in-service inspection and maintenance.

4(4)B

The Eurocodes also require durability against the effects of fatigue. Fatigue design is outside the scope of this guide. For buildings, a fatigue assessment is not normally required except where the members:

a. support lifting appliances or rolling loads
b. are subject to repeated stress cycles from vibrating machinery
c. are subject to wind-induced vibrations
d. are subject to crowd-induced oscillations.

2.5 General requirements for the design of joints

2.5.1 Basic requirements

References given in the margin for Section 2.5 are to BS EN 1991-1-8 and its National Annex unless noted otherwise.

2.2(1)

1. All joints should have a design resistance such that the structure is capable of satisfying all the basic design requirements given in Section 2.1.

2.2(2)

2. The values for the partial factors (γ_{Mi}) are as follows:

NA Tab e N.A.1

▪ Resistance of bolts		γ_{M2}	1.25
▪ Resistance of welds		γ_{M2}	1.25
▪ Resistance of plates in bearing		γ_{M2}	1.25
▪ Slip resistance	at ULS	γ_{M3}	1.25
▪	at SLS	$\gamma_{M3,ser}$	1.10
▪ Preload of high strength bolts		γ_{M7}	1.10

When determining the tying resistance for structural integrity verifications, the following value for the partial factor (γ_{Mi}) should be used:

Tying resistance γ_{Mu} 1.10

2.5.2 Applied forces and moments

2.3(1)

1. The forces and moments applied to joints at the ultimate limit state should be defined according to the principles defined in Section 2.4 and Section 5.

In this context "principles" is understood to include the application rules.

2.5.3 Resistance of joints

2.4(1)

1. The resistance of a joint should be determined on the basis of the resistance of its basic components.

2.4(3)

2. Where fasteners with different stiffnesses are used to carry a shear load the fasteners with the highest stiffness should be designed to carry the design load.

2.5.4 Design assumptions

2.5(1)

1. Joints should be designed on the basis of a realistic assumption of the distribution of internal forces and moments. The following assumptions should be used to determine the distribution of forces:
   a. The internal forces and moments assumed in the analysis are in equilibrium with the forces and moments applied to the joints.
   b. Each element in the joint is capable of resisting the internal forces and moments.
   c. The deformations implied by this distribution do not exceed the deformation capacity of the fasteners or welds and the connected parts.
   d. The assumed distribution of internal forces should be realistic with regard to the relative stiffnesses within the joint.
   e. The deformations assumed in any design model based on elastic-plastic analysis are based on rigid body rotations and/or in-plane deformations which are physically possible.
   f. Any model used is in compliance with the evaluation of test results.

2.5.5 Joints loaded in shear subject to impact, vibration and/or load reversal

> If connections are subject to vibration or similar effects that could lead to bolts becoming loose, the connections are usually arranged with preloaded bolts, locking devices or by welding. Reversal due to wind, or the application and removal of imposed floor loads, is not considered to justify the use of special measures.

2.5.6 Eccentricity at intersections

2.7(1)

1. Where there is eccentricity at intersections, the joints and members should be designed for the resulting moments and forces, except in the case of particular types of structures where it has been demonstrated that it is not necessary, for example hollow section lattice girders (see Section 8.1.2).

> BS EN 1993-1-8 provides guidance in Clause 2.7 on the eccentricities in connections with angles and tees (for example in a truss) when the bolts are not on the centroidal axis of the member.

ACTIONS ON BUILDINGS

References given in the margin for Section 3 are to BS EN 1991-1-1 and its National Annex unless noted otherwise.

3.1 Design situations

3.1(1)P

1.(P) The relevant permanent and imposed loads shall be determined for each design situation.

3.2(1)

2. The total self-weight of structural and non-structural members should be taken into account in combinations of actions as a single action.

3.3.1(1)P

3.(P) For areas which are intended to be subjected to different categories of loadings the design shall consider the most critical load case.

3.3.2(1)

4. On roofs, imposed loads need not be applied in combination with either snow loads or wind actions.

3.2 Densities of construction materials

1. The characteristic values of the densities of construction materials are given in Table 3.1:

Extracted from Tables A.1 and A.4

Table 3.1 Densities of construction materials

Material		Density (kN/m³)
Concrete*	Normal weight	24
	Lightweight, density class LC 2.0	20
	Lightweight, density class LC 1.8	18
Steel		77

***** Add 1 KN/m³ for reinforcement and 1 kN/m³ for wet concrete.**

3.3 Imposed loads

6.1(2)

1. Imposed loads are modelled by uniformly distributed loads, line loads or concentrated loads or combinations of these loads.

6.1(3)

2. For the determination of imposed loads, floor and roof areas in buildings should be sub-divided into categories according to their use.

3.3.1 Load arrrangements

3.3.1.1 *Floors, beams and roofs*

6.2.1(3)P

1.(P) To ensure a minimum local resistance of the floor structure, a separate verification shall be performed with a concentrated load that, unless stated otherwise, shall not be combined with the uniformly distributed loads or other variable actions.

> BS EN 1991-1-1 provides concentrated loads Q_k to be applied over an area of 50 mm x 50 mm, which should be used 'for local verifications'. The uniformly distributed load q_k 'is intended for determination of general effects', and in most cases will govern design.

6.2.1(4), 6.3.1.2(10) and NA.2.5

2. Uniformly distributed imposed loads from a single loading category given in Table 3.2 may be reduced by multiplying it by the following reduction factor:

$$\alpha_A = 1.0 - \frac{A}{1000} \geq 0.75$$

where:

A is the area supported by the member (m²)

Note: ***Loads that have been specifically determined from knowledge of the proposed use of the structure do not qualify for reduction.***

> This note means that the nominal loading for the category of floor may be reduced, as a function of the loaded area supported by a given member (because the probability of a certain level of load being applied over the whole area decreases as that area increases), but not if the loading has been calculated specifically for a given situation.

3.3.1.2 *Columns and walls*

6.2.2(1)

1. For the design of columns or walls, loaded from several storeys, the total imposed loads on the floor of each storey should be assumed to be distributed uniformly.

3.3.2 Characteristic values of imposed loads

1. Imposed load categories and minimum imposed floor loads are given in Table 3.2.
2. Minimum imposed roof loads are given in Table 3.3. See Section 3.4 for snow loads.

Extracted from Tables NA.2 and NA.3

Table 3.2 Categories of loaded areas and minimum imposed floor loads

Category	Example	q_k (kN/m²)
A1	All areas within self-contained single family dwellings or modular student accommodation Communal areas (including kitchens) in blocks of flats that are no more than 2 storeys and only 4 dwellings per floor are accessible from a single staircase.	1.5
A2	Bedrooms and dormitories except those in A1 and A3	1.5
A3	Bedrooms in hotels and motels; hospital wards; toilet areas	2.0

Extracted from Tables NA.2 and NA.3

Table 3.2 (Continued)

Category	Example	q_k (kN/m²)
B1	General office use other than in B2	2.5
B2	Office areas at or below ground floor level	3.0
C31	Corridors, hallways, aisles which are not subjected to crowds or wheeled vehicles and communal areas in blocks of flats not covered by A1	3.0
C51	Areas susceptible to large crowds	5.0
C52	Stages in public assembly areas (see Note 5)	7.5
D	Areas in general retail shops and department stores	4.0

*** Each module has a secure door with no more than six single bedrooms and an internal corridor.**

Minimum imposed floor loads for other areas in categories A to D are given in Table NA.3 of BS EN 1991-1-1 and in Table NA.5 for category E.

Extracted from Table NA.7

Table 3.3 Minimum imposed roof load (roofs not accessible except for normal maintenance and repair)

Roof Slope α (°)	q_k (kN/m²)	Q_k (kN)
$\alpha < 30°$	0.6	
$30° \leq \alpha < 60°$	0.6(60 - α)/30	0.9
$\alpha \geq 60°$	0	

Note: ***All roof slopes α are measured from the horizontal and all loads should be applied vertically.***

3. Imposed roof loads should be treated as independent variable actions, i.e. separate from imposed floor loads and separate from snow loads.

6.3.1.2(11)

4. For columns and walls supporting several storeys of floor areas of categories A–D, the total imposed loads may be reduced by applying the reduction factor α_n.

Table 3.4 Reduction factor for number of storeys

Number of storeys (n)	α_n
$1 \leq n \leq 5$	$1.1 - \frac{n}{10}$
$6 \leq n \leq 10$	0.6
$10 < n$	0.5

NA.2.6

5. Load reductions based on area (see 3.3.1.1(2) above) may be applied if $\alpha_A < \alpha_n$. However, the reductions given by α_A and α_n cannot be used together.

3.3.2(2)

6. When the imposed load is considered as an accompanying action in accordance with BS EN 1990, only one of the two factors ψ and α_n shall be applied.

Note: ***Loads that have been specifically determined from knowledge of the proposed use of the structure do not qualify for reduction.***

3.3.3 Movable partitions

5.1(5)P
5.2.2(2)P
6.3.1.2(8)

1.(P) Loads due to movable partitions shall be treated as imposed loads.

2.(P) For determining the effect of the self-weight due to movable partitions, an equivalent uniformly distributed load shall be used and added to the imposed load, see (3).

3. Provided that a floor allows lateral distribution of loads, the self-weight of movable partitions may be taken into account by a uniformly distributed load (q_k) which should be added to the imposed floor loads obtained from Table 3.2. The uniformly distributed load is dependent on the self-weight of the partitions as follows:
   - for movable partitions with a self-weight ≤ 1.0 kN/m wall length: $q_k = 0.5$ kN/m²
   - for movable partitions with a self-weight ≤ 2.0 kN/m wall length: $q_k = 0.8$ kN/m²
   - for movable partitions with a self-weight ≤ 3.0 kN/m wall length: $q_k = 1.2$ kN/m².

Generally, movable partitions will have a self-weight ≤ 1.0 kN/m thus $q_k = 0.5$ kN/m².

3.3.4 Load arrangement for the design of continuous beams

BS EN 1993-1-1 AB.2(1)B

1. For continuous beams with slabs in buildings without cantilevers on which uniformly distributed loads are dominant, it is sufficient to consider only the following load arrangements.
   a. alternative spans carrying the design permanent and variable load ($\gamma_G G_k + \gamma_Q Q_k$), other spans carrying only the design permanent load $\gamma_G G_k$
   b. any two adjacent spans carrying the design permanent and variable loads ($\gamma_G G_k + \gamma_Q Q_k$), all other spans carrying only the design permanent load $\gamma_G G_k$

Note: ***(a) results in maximum practical sagging moments, (b) results in maximum practical hogging moments.***

3.4 Snow loads

Refer to BS EN 1991-1-3 and its National Annex for snow loads on buildings.

The characteristic ground snow load varies by location, and altitude, so this data must be known to enable an accurate calculation to be made.

The characteristic snow load is multiplied by a factor μ which allows for the roof slope and exposure and thermal factors (C_e and C_t - both normally set to 1.0).

The UK National Annex specifies that the design situations and load conditions to be used should be taken from Case B2 of Table A.1. This means that the design situations are:

- undrifted snow
- drifted snow (partial removal of snow from one slope)
- drifted snow (behind parapets, in valleys, from higher buildings etc, as covered by Annex B of BS EN 1991-1-3).

The first two situations are to be considered as persistent situations (and so should be used in combination with other actions using expression 6.10, 6.10a and 6.10b). The third situation is to be considered as an accidental situation, to be combined with other actions using expression 6.11b.

3.5 Wind actions

Refer to BS EN 1991-1-4 and its National Annex for wind actions on buildings.

Designers should pay careful attention to the requirements covering internal pressures. In Clause 7.2.9(6) the Eurocode allows an internal pressure coefficient to be calculated, based on permeability, or for designers to consider internal pressure coefficients of +0.2 and –0.3.

Specific guidance is given (Clause 7.2.9(3)) when dominant openings are considered to be shut at ULS – the accidental situation of them being open must also be considered.

3.6 Actions on structures during execution

Refer to BS EN 1991-1-6 and its National Annex for actions during execution (construction).

4.11.1(1) 1. Variable construction loads (Q_k) may be considered as one single variable action, or where appropriate different types of construction load may be combined and applied as a single variable action.

Based on the design principles given in BS EN 1991-1-6, the SCI recommends the following for determining construction loads.

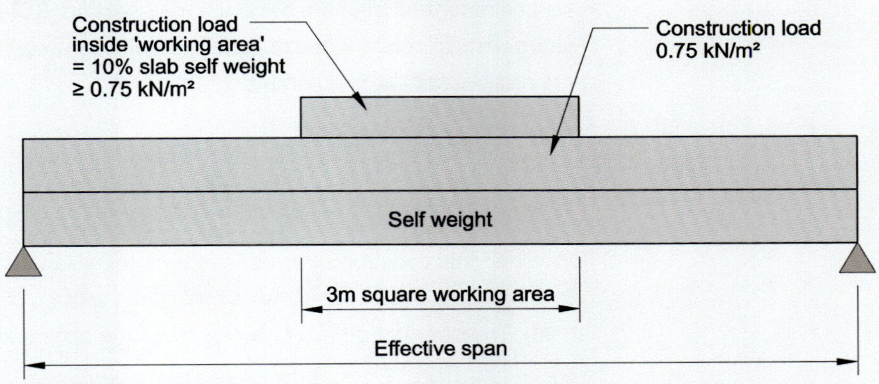

Actions for design of decking

The working area should be considered to be a patch load of area 3 m × 3 m. This area should be applied in its most onerous location.

Concrete in its wet state should be considered as a variable action. However, reinforcing bars should be considered to be permanent actions.

The following combination of actions is recommended for the execution stage:

$$1.35\,G_{k,1a} + 1.5\,Q_{k,1a} + 1.5\,Q_{k,1b} + 1.5\,Q_{k1c}$$

where:

$G_{k,1a}$ is the permanent action (self weight of decking and reinforcement).

$Q_{k,1a}$ is the variable action for personnel and heaping of concrete, etc. in the working area (typically 0.75 kN/m²).

$Q_{k,1b}$	is the variable action for personnel etc. across the full area 0.75 kN/m^2).
$Q_{k,1c}$	is the variable action (wet concrete) applied across the full area, including additional concrete from ponding where applicable.

The additional loads due to ponding must be included when checking the resistance if the deflection exceeds 10% of the slab depth. When determining the deflection of the metal deck due to ponding for this check, the following combination of actions should be considered:

$$1.0\,G_{k,1a} + 1.0\,Q_{k,1c}$$

EN 1994-1-1 9.6(2) describes this combination in words as: 'the deflection of the sheeting (should be checked) under its own weight plus the weight of wet concrete, excluding the construction load'.

Guidance on the limiting deflection under the weight of wet concrete and self weight of the profile is given in the UK NA, which recommends the lesser of the effective span/180 and 20 mm as the limit when loads from ponding are ignored, and the lesser of the effective span/130 and 30 mm when loads from ponding are included. It is worth noting that this guidance assumes the slab is cast to a constant thickness over the supporting beams. The self-weight of concrete will vary depending on the method of levelling that is adopted on site.

For the verification of the SLS deflection during the execution of a building, as well as deformation of the decking cross-section, SCI recommends that the characteristic combination of actions should be used because deformations may be irreversible, with $\psi_0 = 1.0$ and $\psi_2 = 0.2$:

$$G_{k,1a} + Q_{k,1a} + Q_{k,1b} + Q_{k,1c}$$

Where $G_{k,1b}$ is the self-weight of the beam, and the other symbols are defined above.

Provided that construction is adequately supervised, SCI recommends that $Q_{k,1a}$ may be taken as 0.0 (so beams may be designed without consideration of a moving patch load). The designer should however make the contractor aware of this assumption.

When allowance for ponding is included in the decking verification, (in $Q_{k,1c}$) it should be included in the beam verification.

When determining the deflection of a beam during the execution stage of a building the following combination of actions should be considered:

$$1.0G_{k,1a} + 1.0G_{k,1b} + 1.0Q_{k,1c}$$

Actions for design of beams supporting composite floors

The following combination of actions is recommended for the verification of a composite beam during execution:

$$1.35G_{k,1a} + 1.35G_{k,1b} + 1.5Q_{k,1b} + 1.5Q_{k,1c}$$

3.7 Accidental actions

1991-1-3 Table A.1

1. The drifted snow load arrangements determined using Annex B of BS EN 1991-1-3 should be treated as accidental design situations.

3.7.1 Robustness

References given in the margin for Section 3.7.1 are to BS EN 1991-1-7 and its National Annex unless noted otherwise.

> Guidance on meeting the robustness requirements in Approved Document A is given in SCI publication P341.

3.7.1.1 Vertical ties

A.6(1)

1. Each column and wall should be tied continuously from the foundations to the roof level.

A.6(2)

2. Columns and walls carrying vertical actions should be capable of resisting an accidental design tensile force equal to the largest design vertical permanent and variable load reaction applied to the column from any one floor. Such accidental design loading should not be assumed to act simultaneously with permanent and variable actions that may be acting on the structure.

3.7.1.2 Horizontal ties

A.5.1(1)

1. Horizontal ties should be provided around the perimeter of each floor and roof level and internally in two right angle directions. At least 30% of the ties should be located in the close vicinity of the grid lines of the building.

A.5.1(3)

2. Each horizontal tie should be capable of resisting the following forces:

Internal ties $T_i = 0.8\ (g_k + \psi q_k)\ sL$ or 75 kN whichever is the greater

Perimeter ties $T_p = 0.4\ (g_k + \psi q_k)\ sL$ or 75 kN whichever is the greater

where:

s is the spacing of the ties

L is the length of the tie

ψ is the combination coefficient relevant to the accidental design action being considered (ψ_1 or ψ_2).

3.7.1.3 Key elements

A.8(1)

1. A "key element" should be capable of sustaining an accidental design action (A_d) of 34 kN/m^2 applied in the horizontal and vertical directions (in one direction at a time) to the member and any attached components.

A.8(1)

2. When verifying the resistance of the key element the ultimate strength of the components and their connections should be used.

MATERIALS

References given in the margin for Section 4 are to BS EN 1993-1-1 and its National Annex, unless otherwise stated

4.1 Structural steel

4.1.1 Scope

Based on 3.1(2)

1. This publication covers steel conforming to BS EN 10025 and in BS EN 10210 in grades S275, S355 and S460.

> BS EN 1993-1-1 covers steel conforming to BS EN 10025 Parts 2, 3, 4, 5 and 6, BS EN 10210-1 and BS EN 10219-1 in grades S235 to S460. S355 is currently the only grade in common use for rolled sections in the UK, although there is growing interest in S460. Cold formed sections are not covered in this guide.

4.1.2 Material properties for hot rolled steel

4.1.2.1 Nominal values

3.1(1) and 3.2.1(1)

1. Table 4.1 gives nominal values of the yield strength (f_y) and the ultimate tensile strength (f_u), which should be adopted as characteristic values.

NA.2.4

Table 4.1 Nominal values of yield strength (f_y) and ultimate tensile strength (f_u)

Steel grade and sub-grade	f_y (N/mm²) Nominal thickness of element t (mm)						f_u (N/mm²) Nominal thickness t (mm)	
	$t \le 16$	$16 < t \le 40$	$40 < t \le 63$	$63 < t \le 80$	$80 < t \le 100$	$100 < t \le 150$	$3 \le t \le 100$	$100 < t \le 150$
S275JR								
S275J0	275	265	255	245	235	225	410	400
S275J2								
S355JR	355	345	335	325	315	295	470	450
S355JO								
S355J2								
S355K2								
S355J0H	355	345	335	325	315	295	470	450
S355J2H								
S355K2H								

Table 4.1 (Continued) Nominal values of yield strength (f_y) and ultimate tensile strength (f_u)

Steel grade and sub-grade	f_y (N/mm²) Nominal thickness of element t (mm)						f_u (N/mm²) Nominal thickness of element t (mm)				
	$t \leq 16$	$16 < t \leq 40$	$40 < t \leq 63$	$63 < t \leq 80$	$80 < t \leq 100$	$100 < t \leq 150$	$t \leq 40$	$40 < t \leq 63$	$63 < t \leq 80$	$80 < t \leq 100$	$100 < t \leq 150$
S460N S460NL	460	440	430	410	400	380	540	540	540	540	530
S460M S460ML	460	440	430	410	400	385	540	530	510	500	490

Note 1: *As stated in the National Annex to BS EN 1993-1-1, NA.2.4, for designs in the UK the ultimate strength f_u should be taken as the lowest value of the range given (in the Product Standard). This minimum value is quoted above.*

Note 2: *Although not stated in the Eurocodes, for rolled sections, t may be taken as the flange thickness.*

4.1.2.2 Ductility

3.2.2(2)

1. For steels, a minimum ductility, expressed in terms of limits for the ratio f_u / f_y is required. Steel grades given in Table 4.1 should be considered as satisfying the requirements for ductility.

4.1.2.3 Fracture toughness

3.2.3(1)

1. The material should have sufficient fracture toughness to avoid brittle fracture at the lowest service temperature.

PD 66951-1-10 2.2

2. For buildings in the UK the lowest service temperatures should be taken as −5 °C for internal steel work and −15 °C for external steelwork.

Note: ***This guide does not cover the requirements for toughness for use of steel in other than the normal range of ambient conditions for buildings; use in cold stores, for example, is not covered - refer to the BS EN 1993-1-10 for more detailed guidance.***

3.2.3(1)

3. To avoid brittle fracture, the steel thicknesses should not exceed the maximum permissible values given in Table 4.4(a) or Table 4.4(b) (for structures subject to fatigue), or Table 4.4(c) or Table 4.4(d) (for so-called quasi-static structures). These tables can be used for internal steelwork or external steelwork.

4. The following steps should be used to determine the maximum permissible steel thickness.

   - Classify the detail in terms of temperature adjustment ΔT_{Rd}, see (5).
   - Calculate the maximum tensile stress at the detail $\frac{\sigma_{Ed}}{f_y(t)}$; where $f_y(t)$ is obtained from Table 4.1 for the steel grade and thickness, and σ_{Ed} should be calculated as for the serviceability limit state.

- Select the relevant column in Table 4.4 according to the combination of values of ΔT_{Rd}, and the maximum tensile stress.

Note: ***Each column in Table 4.4, labelled Comb.1, Comb.2 etc, represents combinations of ΔT_{Rd}, and maximum tensile stress which have the same requirement for toughness.***

- Verify the conditions assumed in Note 1 of Table 4.4. In the event that a parameter is not equal to zero, move from the relevant column to a new column. For each 10°C adjustment of ΔT a movement of one column to the right should be made.
- Select the lowest Charpy subgrade, appropriate to the steel grade, for which the maximum thickness in the selected column is equal to or greater than that of the element being considered (usually the flange).

5. $\Delta T_{Rd} = 0°C$, except as follows:

a. *Unwelded details*
For unwelded as-rolled, ground or machined surfaces, $\Delta T_{Rd} = +30°C$.
For unwelded mechanically fastened joints or flame cut edges, $\Delta T_{Rd} = +20°C$.

b. *Welded details*
For welded details, the values given in Table 4.2 should be used.

BS EN 1993-1-10
NA.2.1.1.2

Table 4.2 Values of ΔT_{Rd} for specific weld locations

Component or detail	Initiation Site	Attachment dimensions[1] Length[2] (mm)	Attachment dimensions[1] Width[3] (mm)	ΔT_{Rd} (°C)
Welded attachment	Transverse weld toe	>150	≤ 50 >50	-20 -30
Member fabricated from plates	Transverse butt weld[4]	None	None	-20
Rolled sections	Transverse butt weld[4]	None	None	-30

1 Measured overall between weld toes on member concerned.
2 Measured in direction of tensile stress.
3 Measured transverse to direction of tensile stress.
4 Applies only to welds joining the full cross section, not those joining individual plates prior to sub-assembly.

Note: ***In Table 4.4 the three rows for $\Delta T_{Rd} = 0°C$ $-20°C$ and $-30°C$ are referred to as Welded - moderate, Welded - severe and Welded - very severe respectively. The row for $\Delta T_{Rd} = +20°C$ is referred to as Bolted, although it also covers unwelded flame cut edges.***

BS EN 1993-1-10
NA.2.1.1.2
BS EN 1993-1-10
Table NA.2

6. Where geometry is likely to result in the occurrence of areas of gross stress concentrations, the value of ΔT_{Rg}, should be obtained from Table 4.3.

Table 4.3 Values of ΔT_{Rg} for stress concentration factors

Stress concentration factor (k_f)	ΔT_{Rg} (°C)
1	0
1.5	-10
2	-20
3	-30

The above stress concentration factors are not applicable for bolt holes.

Note: *For buildings within the scope of this guide, details that would require evaluation of a stress concentration factor include large holes, re-entrant corners and the welding of a beam flange to an unstiffened column. Conservatively an adjustment of $\Delta T_{Rg} = -30°C$ could be made in such cases. For holes and re-entrant corners, a more detailed evaluation can be made in accordance with PD 6695-1-9. For beams welded to unstiffened columns, the stress concentration factor can be determined from:*

$$k_f = \frac{b_b}{b_{eff}}$$

where:

b_b is the width of the beam

b_{eff} is the effective width $b_{eff} = t_{w,c} + 2(r + 2t_{f,c})$

$t_{w,c}$ is the web thickness of the column

$t_{f,c}$ is the flange thickness of the column

Figure 4.1 Stress concentration in a beam-to-column welded connection without column stiffeners (only top flange shown)

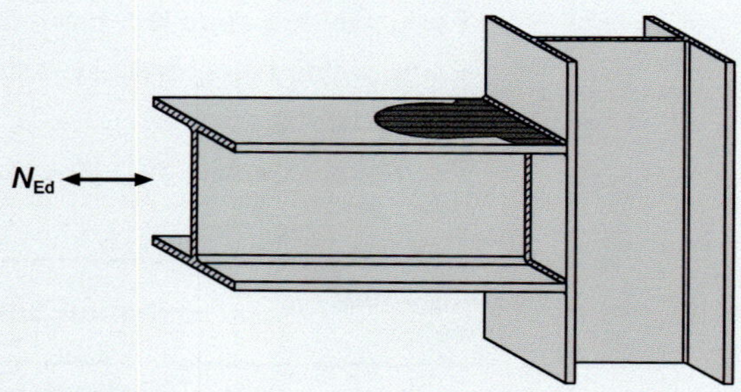

BS EN 1993-1-10 2.3.1(2)

7. The values given in Table 4.4 assume a reference strain rate of $\dot{\varepsilon}_0 = 4 \times 10^{-4}$/sec, for which $\Delta T_{\dot{\varepsilon}} = 0$. Dynamic action effects for most transient and persistent design situations are covered by this strain rate. For other strain rates $\dot{\varepsilon}$ (e.g. for impact loads) $\Delta T_{\dot{\varepsilon}}$ should be determined from:

$$\Delta T_{\dot{\varepsilon}} = -\frac{1440 - f_y(t)}{550}\left(\ln\frac{\dot{\varepsilon}}{\dot{\varepsilon}_0}\right)^{1.5}$$

Conservatively, a value of $\Delta T_{\dot{\varepsilon}} = -30°C$ may be used for buildings where vehicle impact on a member has to be considered.

PD 6695-1-10, 2.2

P419

Note: *Table 4.4(a) and Table 4.4(b) are taken from PD 6695-1-10, which should be used for structures subject to fatigue. Table 4.4(c) and Table 4.4(d) present values that were derived using the same approach but recognising that in quasi-static structures initial cracks will not grow. Use of the tables is described in paragraphs (4) to (7) below. Values are taken from Brittle fracture: Selection of steel sub-grade to BS EN 1993-1-10 (SCI publication P419) and a worked example showing the steps is given in Steel building design: Worked examples - Open sections (SCI publication P364). The scope of application is limited to details that fall within the scope of BS EN 1993-1-9*

Extracted from PD 6695-1-10 Table 2

Table 4.4(a) Maximum thicknesses for internal steelwork in structures subject to fatigue[1]

Detail Type		Tensile stress level, $\sigma_{Ed}/f_y(t)$ [2]									
Description	ΔT_{RD}	**Comb. 1**	**Comb. 2**	**Comb. 3**	**Comb. 4**	**Comb. 5**	**Comb. 6**	**Comb. 7**	**Comb. 8**	**Comb. 9**	**Comb. 10**
Plain material	+30°	≤ 0	0.15	0.3	≥0.5						
Bolted	+20°		≤ 0	0.15	0.3	≥0.5					
Welded - moderate	0°				≤ 0	0.15	0.3	≥0.5			
Welded - severe	-20°						≤ 0	0.15	0.3	≥0.5	
Welded - very severe	-30°							≤ 0	0.15	0.3	≥0.5

		Maximum thickness (mm) according to combination of stress level and detail type									
Steel Grade	**Sub-grade**	**Comb. 1**	**Comb. 2**	**Comb. 3**	**Comb. 4**	**Comb. 5**	**Comb. 6**	**Comb. 7**	**Comb. 8**	**Comb. 9**	**Comb. 10**
		Internal Steelwork $T_{md} = -5°C$									
S275	JR	122.5	102.5	85	70	60	50	40	32.5	27.5	22.5
	JO	192.5	172.5	147.5	122.5	102.5	85	70	60	50	40
	J2	200	200	192.5	172.5	147.5	122.5	102.5	85	70	60
	M, N	200	200	200	192.5	172.5	147.5	122.5	102.5	85	70
	ML, NL	200	200	200	200	200	192.5	172.5	147.5	122.5	102.5
S355	JR	82.5	67.5	55	45	37.5	30	22.5	17.5	15	12.5
	JO	142.5	120	100	82.5	67.5	55	45	37.5	30	22.5
	J2	190	167.5	142.5	120	100	82.5	67.5	55	45	37.5
	K2, M, N	200	190	167.5	142.5	120	100	82.5	67.5	55	45
	ML, NL	200	200	200	190	167.5	142.5	120	100	82.5	67.5
S460	Q	137.5	115	97.5	80	65	55	45	35	27.5	22.5
	M, N	162.5	137.5	115	97.5	80	65	55	45	35	27.5
	Q, L	187.5	162.5	137.5	115	97.5	80	65	55	45	35
	ML, NL	200	187.5	162.5	137.5	115	97.5	80	65	55	45
	QL1	200	200	181.5	162.5	137.5	115	97.5	80	65	55

Notes:

[1] *This Table is based on the following conditions:*

- $\Delta T_{Rg} = 0$, *See 4.1.2.3(5)*
- $\Delta T_{\dot{\varepsilon}} = 0$, *See 4.1.2.3(7)*

If either of conditions i. or ii. are not complied with, an appropriate adjustment towards the right side of the table should be made in accordance with 4.1.2.3(4).

[2] $f_y(t)$ *should be obtained from Table 4.1.*

Extracted from PD 6695-1-10 Table 3

Table 4.4(b) Maximum thicknesses for external steelwork in structures subject to fatigue[1]

Detail Type		Tensile stress level, $\sigma_{Ed}/f_y(t)$ [2]									
Description	ΔT_{RD}	Comb. 1	Comb. 2	Comb. 3	Comb. 4	Comb. 5	Comb. 6	Comb. 7	Comb. 8	Comb. 9	Comb. 10
Plain material	+30°	≤ 0	0.15	0.3	≥0.5						
Bolted	+20°		≤ 0	0.15	0.3	≥0.5					
Welded - moderate	0°				≤ 0	0.15	0.3	≥0.5			
Welded - severe	-20°						≤ 0	0.15	0.3	≥0.5	
Welded - very severe	-30°							≤ 0	0.15	0.3	≥0.5

Steel Grade	Sub-grade	Maximum thickness (mm) according to combination of stress level and detail type									
		Comb. 1	Comb. 2	Comb. 3	Comb. 4	Comb. 5	Comb. 6	Comb. 7	Comb. 8	Comb. 9	Comb. 10
		External Steelwork $T_{md} = -15°C$									
S275	JR	70	60	50	40	32.5	27.5	22.5	17.5	12.5	10
	JO	172.5	147.5	122.5	102.5	85	70	60	50	40	32.5
	J2	200	192.5	172.5	147.5	122.5	102.5	85	70	60	50
	M, N	200	200	192.5	172.5	147.5	122.5	102.5	85	70	60
	ML, NL	200	200	200	200	192.5	172.5	147.5	122.5	102.5	85
S355	JR	45	37.5	30	22.5	17.5	15	12.5	10	7.5	5
	JO	120	100	82.5	67.5	55	45	37.5	30	22.5	17.5
	J2	167.5	142.5	120	100	82.5	37.5	55	45	37.5	30
	K2, M, N	190	167.5	142.5	120	100	82.5	67.5	55	45	37.5
	ML, NL	200	200	190	167.5	142.5	120	100	82.5	67.5	55
S460	Q	115	97.5	80	65	55	45	35	27.5	22.5	17.5
	M, N	137.5	115	97.5	80	65	55	45	35	27.5	22.5
	Q, L	162.5	137.5	115	97.5	80	65	55	45	35	27.5
	ML, NL	187.5	162.5	137.5	115	97.5	80	65	55	45	35
	QL1	200	187.5	162.5	137.5	115	97.5	80	65	55	45

Notes:

[1] *This Table is based on the following conditions:*

- $\Delta T_{Rg} = 0$, *See 4.1.2.3(5)*
- $\Delta T_{\dot{\varepsilon}} = 0$, *See 4.1.2.3(7)*

If either of conditions i. or ii. are not complied with, an appropriate adjustment towards the right side of the table should be made in accordance with 4.1.2.3(4).

[2] $f_y(t)$ *should be obtained from Table 4.1.*

Table 4.4(c)   Maximum thicknesses for internal steelwork in quasi-static structures [1]

Detail Type		Tensile stress level, $\sigma_{Ed}/f_y(t)$ [2]									
Description	ΔT_{RD}	**Comb. 1**	**Comb. 2**	**Comb. 3**	**Comb. 4**	**Comb. 5**	**Comb. 6**	**Comb. 7**	**Comb. 8**	**Comb. 9**	**Comb. 10**
Plain material	+30°	≤ 0	0.15	0.3	≥0.5						
Bolted	+20°		≤ 0	0.15	0.3	≥0.5					
Welded - moderate	0°				≤ 0	0.15	0.3	≥0.5			
Welded - severe	-20°						≤ 0	0.15	0.3	≥0.5	
Welded - very severe	-30°							≤ 0	0.15	0.3	≥0.5

		Maximum thickness (mm) according to combination of stress level and detail type									
Steel Grade	**Sub-grade**	**Comb. 1**	**Comb. 2**	**Comb. 3**	**Comb. 4**	**Comb. 5**	**Comb. 6**	**Comb. 7**	**Comb. 8**	**Comb. 9**	**Comb. 10**
		Internal Steelwork $T_{md} = -5°C$									
S275	JR	200	200	200	200	200	200	200	166.5	112	77.5
	JO	200	200	200	200	200	200	200	200	200	200
	J2	200	200	200	200	200	200	200	200	200	200
	M, N	200	200	200	200	200	200	200	200	200	200
	ML, NL	200	200	200	200	200	200	200	200	200	200
S355	JR	200	200	200	200	188.5	145.5	95.5	65.5	47	35
	JO	200	200	200	200	200	200	200	188.5	145.5	95.5
	J2	200	200	200	200	200	200	200	200	200	188.5
	K2, M, N	200	200	200	200	200	200	200	200	200	200
	ML, NL	200	200	200	200	200	200	200	200	200	200
S460	Q	200	200	200	200	200	200	200	173.5	121.5	80.5
	M, N	200	200	200	200	200	200	200	200	173.5	121.5
	Q, L	200	200	200	200	200	200	200	200	200	173.5
	ML, NL	200	200	200	200	200	200	200	200	200	200
	QL1	200	200	200	200	200	200	200	200	200	200

Notes:

[1] *This Table is based on the following conditions:*

- $\Delta T_{Rg} = 0$, *See 4.1.2.3(5)*
- $\Delta T_{\dot{\varepsilon}} = 0$, *See 4.1.2.3(7)*

If either of conditions i. or ii. are not complied with, an appropriate adjustment towards the right side of the table should be made in accordance with 4.1.2.3(4).

[2] $f_y(t)$ *should be obtained from Table 4.1.*

4.1.2.4 Through-thickness properties

3.2.4 refers to EN 1993-1-10 and to the NA. PD 6695-1-10 presents an alternative set of simple rules.

1. For low and medium risk situations, through thickness properties do not need to be specified.

2. For guidance on fabrication control measures for areas of low and medium high risk, see PD 6695-1-10, Clause 3.2.

3. For areas at high risk of the occurrence of lamellar tearing Z35 quality steel should be specified for the 'through' material.

PD 6695-1-10 3.3

4. The following areas are considered as high-risk

- Tee joints where $t_z > 35$ mm
- Cruciform joints where $t_z > 25$ mm
- Corner joints where the 'through' material is not prepared and $t_z > 20$ mm

where:

t_z is either:
The thickness of the 'incoming' material for butt welds and deep penetration fillet welds, or
The throat size of the largest fillet weld.

Note: *In Tee and cruciform joints, 'incoming' elements are welded to the surface of 'through' elements, either by fillet welds or by butt welds (then the incoming element usually has a weld preparation). In corner joints, the incoming element is either welded to the surface of the through element or the through element is prepared, as shown in Figure 4.2*

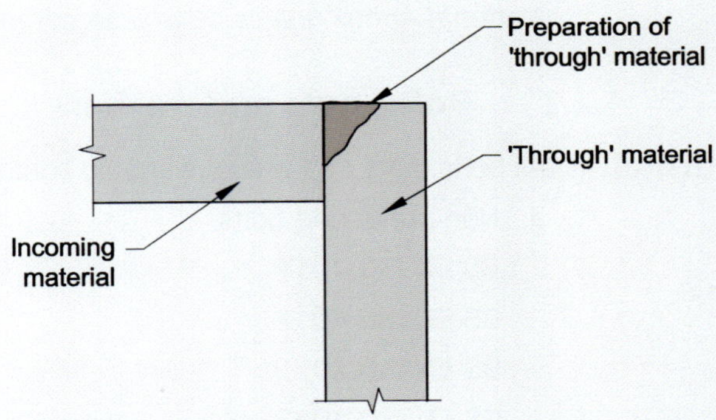

Figure 4.2 Preparation of a corner joint

5. In high risk areas the following are also recommended:

- Do not over-specify the weld throat size.
- Reduce the weld volume to a minimum. In heavy tee/cruciform joints, double partial penetration butt welds with reinforcing fillet welds may be preferable to full penetration butt welds or large fillet welds (provided that fatigue through the throat is not the governing mode of failure).

4.1.2.5 Tolerances

3.2.5(1) 1. The dimension and mass tolerances of rolled steel sections and plates should conform to the relevant product standard.

> Relevant product standards include:
> - BS EN 10365 (for I and H sections and channels)
> - BS EN 10056 (for angle sections)
> - BS EN 10210 (for hot finished hollow sections).

3.2.5(2) 2. For welded components the tolerances given in BS EN 1090 should be applied.

3.2.5(3) 3. For structural analysis and design the nominal values of dimensions should be used.

4.1.2.6 Design values of material coefficients

3.2.6(1) 1. The values of material properties that should be used for structural steel design to this document are:

- Modulus of Elasticity $E = 210{,}000 \text{ N/mm}^2$
- Shear modulus $G = \dfrac{E}{2(1+\nu)} \approx 81{,}000 \text{ N/ mm}^2$
- Poisson's ratio in elastic stage $\nu = 0.3$

4.2 Connecting devices

References given in the margin for Section 4.2 are to BS EN 1993-1-8 and its National Annex unless otherwise noted.

4.2.1 Bolts, nuts and washers

Based on 3.1.1(1) and Group 4 Reference Standards, BS EN 1993-1-8, 1.2.4

1. All bolts, nuts and washers should conform to the following reference standards:

   a. Non-preloaded bolts

      BS EN ISO 4014
      BS EN ISO 4017
      BS EN ISO 4032
      BS EN ISO 4033
      BS EN ISO 7089
      BS EN ISO 7090
      BS 4190

   b. Preloaded bolts

      BS EN 14399-1
      BS EN 14399-2
      BS EN 14399-3
      BS EN 14399-5
      BS EN 14399-6
      BS EN 14399-9
      BS EN 14399-10

3.1.1(2) NA.2.4 — 2. The rules given in this guide cover the use of bolt classes 4.6, 8.8 and 10.9.

3.1.1(3) — 3. The nominal values for yield strength f_{yb} and ultimate tensile strength f_{ub} are given in Table 4.5. These values should be taken as the characteristic values in design calculations.

Extracted from Table 3.1

Table 4.5 Nominal values of yield strength f_{yb} and ultimate tensile strength f_{ub} for bolts

Bolt Class	4.6	8.8	10.9
f_{yb} (N/mm²)	240	640	900
f_{ub} (N/mm²)	400	800	1000

In the UK, non-preloaded bolts are usually Class 8.8.

3.1.2(1) — 4. Only bolt assemblies of Class 8.8 and Class 10.9 conforming to the reference standards given in (1) with controlled tightening in accordance with BS EN 1090-2 may be used as preloaded bolts.

In the UK, only system HR and system HRC bolts are used as preloaded bolts. System HV bolts (to BS EN 14399-4) are not used in the UK.

4.2.2 Welding consumables

4.2(1) — 1. All welding consumables should conform to the relevant standards given in BS EN 1090-2.

There are no reference standards for welding consumables in BS EN 1993-1-8.

4.2(2) — 2. The specified yield strength, ultimate tensile strength, elongation at failure and minimum Charpy V-notch energy value of the filler metal should be equivalent to, or better than, that specified for the parent material.

UK practice is to use welding consumables which are appropriate to achieve the above requirement for all grades of structural steel.

4.3 Other products in buildings

3.4(1) — 1. Any structural components used in the design of a building structure should comply with the relevant product Standard or ETAG or ETA.

4.4 Concrete

1. The rules in this guide cover the use of the concrete grades given in Table 4.6 and Table 4.7.

Extracted from BS EN 1992-1-1 Table 3.1

Table 4.6 Normal concrete material properties

		C25/30	C30/37	C35/45	C40/50
Cylinder strength (MPa)	f_{ck}	25	30	35	40
Cube strength (MPa)	$f_{ck,cube}$	30	37	45	50
Secant modulus of elasticity (GPa)	E_{cm}	31	33	34	35

Extracted from BS EN 1992-1-1 Table 11.3.1

Table 4.7 Light weight concrete material properties

		LC25/28	LC30/33	LC35/38
Cylinder strength (MPa)	f_{ck}	25	30	35
Cube strength (MPa)	$f_{ck,cube}$	28	33	38
Secant modulus of elasticity (GPa) E_{lcm}	E_{lcm}		$E_{lcm} = E_{cm}\,\eta_E$	

Notes:

E_{cm} *is given by Table 4.6 for the corresponding value of* f_{ck}

η_E $= (p/2200)^2$ *where* p *denotes the oven-dry density in accordance with BS EN 206-1 Section 4.*

CALCULATION OF INTERNAL FORCES AND MOMENTS

References given in the margin for Section 5 are to BS EN 1993-1-1 and its National Annex, unless otherwise stated.

5.1 Structural modelling

5.1.1(2) 1. The calculation model and basic assumptions for the calculations should reflect the structural behaviour at the relevant limit state with appropriate accuracy and reflect the anticipated type of behaviour of the cross sections, members, joints and bearings.

Generally, analysis models may include the base stiffness, connection stiffness and an allowance for the inevitable imperfections present within a structure (see Section 5.3). UK practice is generally not to allow for *member* imperfections in the analysis model, since these are automatically allowed for when determining member resistances in accordance with Section 6.

Base stiffness is covered by NCCI SN045 (available from www.steel-ncci.com). For a nominally pinned base 10% of the column stiffness $\left(\frac{EI}{L}\right)$ may be assumed when calculating frame stability, and 20% at SLS.

UK practice is generally to consider connections as either pinned or rigid, and then to ensure that the connection details realise these assumptions.

5.2 Effects of deformed geometry of the structure

5.2.1(1) 1. The internal forces and moments may generally be determined using either:

- first-order analysis, using the initial geometry of the structure, or
- second-order analysis, taking into account the influence of the deformation of the structure.

5.2.1(2) 2. The effects of the deformed geometry (second order effects) should be considered if they increase the action effects significantly or modify significantly the structural behaviour.

5.2.1(3) 3. First order analysis may be used for the structure, if the increase of the relevant internal forces or moments or any other change of structural behaviour caused by deformations can be neglected. This may be assumed to be fulfilled, if the following criterion is satisfied:

$$\alpha_{cr} = \frac{F_{cr}}{F_{Ed}} \geq 10$$ for elastic analysis

$$\alpha_{cr} = \frac{F_{cr}}{F_{Ed}} \geq 15$$ for plastic analysis

where:

α_{cr} is the factor by which the loading would have to be increased to cause elastic instability in a global mode

F_{Ed} is the design loading on the structure

F_{cr} is the elastic critical buckling load for the global instability model based on initial elastic stiffnesses.

NA.2.9

Note that according to the UK NA, a less conservative limit may be used for plastic analysis:

$$\alpha_{cr} = \frac{F_{cr}}{F_{Ed}} \geq 10$$ for clad structures provided that the stiffening effect of panels and walls is not taken into account.

$$\alpha_{cr} = \frac{F_{cr}}{F_{Ed}} \geq 5$$ for frames subject to gravity load combinations only, and satisfying the following geometrical constraints:

- The span, L, does not exceed 5 times the mean height of the columns.
- h_r satisfies the criterion:

  $$(h_r/s_a)^2 + (h_r/s_b)^2 \leq 0.5$$

  in which s_a and s_b are the horizontal distances from the apex to the columns. For a symmetrical frame this expression simplifies to $h_r \leq 0.25L$.

5.2.1(4)B

4. Beam-and-column type plane frames in buildings may be checked for sway mode failure with first order analysis if the criterion (5.1) is satisfied for each storey. In these structures α_{cr} may be calculated using the following approximate formula, provided that the axial compression in the beams or rafters is not significant:

5.2

$$\alpha_{cr} = \left(\frac{H_{Ed}}{V_{Ed}}\right)\left(\frac{h}{\delta_{H,Ed}}\right)$$

where:

H_{Ed} is the design value of the horizontal reaction at the bottom of the storey of the horizontal loads and equivalent horizontal forces representing the effects of sway imperfections (see 5.3.2)

V_{Ed} is the total design vertical load on the structure on the bottom of the storey

$\delta_{H,Ed}$ is the horizontal displacement at the top of the storey, relative to the bottom of the storey, when the frame is loaded with horizontal loads (e.g. wind) and the equivalent horizontal forces which are applied at each floor level

h is the storey height.

The calculation of α_{cr} may often be based on the analysis of a single bracing system. In that case, the applied loads H_{Ed} and V_{Ed} should be the proportion of the total loads carried by that bracing system.

The above expression 5.2 is not appropriate for portal frames. A modified expression for portal frames, $\alpha_{cr,est}$ should be calculated, following the recommended approach in Lim, *et al. 'Eurocode 3 and the in-plane stability of portal frames'* (The Structural Engineer, November 2005). This approach is adopted in *Design of steel portal frame buildings to Eurocode 3* (SCI publication P399).

5.3 Imperfections

5.3.1 Basis

5.3.1(1) 1. Appropriate allowances should be incorporated in the structural analysis to cover the effects of imperfections, including residual stresses and geometrical imperfections such as lack of verticality, lack of straightness, lack of flatness, lack of fit and any minor eccentricities present in joints of the unloaded structure.

5.3.1(3) 2. The following imperfections should be taken into account:

a. global imperfections for frames and bracing systems

b. local imperfections for individual members

5.3.4(1) Global imperfections may be taken into account by modelling the frame out of plumb, or by a series of equivalent horizontal forces applied to a frame modelled vertically. The latter approach is recommended. Imperfections in individual members may be modelled, or members may be modelled as straight and imperfections automatically allowed for by verifying member resistances in accordance with Section 6. The latter approach is recommended, so no detailed advice on modelling individual member imperfections is given in this guide.

5.3.2 Imperfections for global analysis of frames

5.3.2(1) 1. The assumed shape of global imperfections and local imperfections may be derived from the elastic buckling mode of a structure in the plane of buckling considered.

5.3.2(2) 2. Both in and out-of-plane buckling with symmetric and asymmetric buckling shapes should be taken into account in the most unfavourable direction and form.

5.3.2(3) 3. For frames sensitive to buckling in a sway mode the effect of imperfections should be allowed for in frame analysis by means of an equivalent imperfection in the form of an initial sway imperfection. The initial sway imperfections (See Figure 5.1) may be determined from:

$$\phi = \phi_0 \, \alpha_h \, \alpha_m$$

where:

ϕ_0 = 1/200

α_h is the reduction factor for height h applicable to columns:

$= \frac{2}{\sqrt{h}}$ but $\frac{2}{3} \leq \alpha_h \leq 1.0$

h is the height of the structure in metres

α_m is the reduction factor for the number of columns in a row

$= \sqrt{0.5(1+1/m)}$

m is the number of vertical members contributing to the horizontal force on the bracing system.

Note that the above definition of m has been taken from BS EN 1992-1-1 Clause 5.2(6) as a more appropriate definition than that in BS EN 1993, which refers to the "number of columns in a row". Typical buildings do not have bracing in every row.

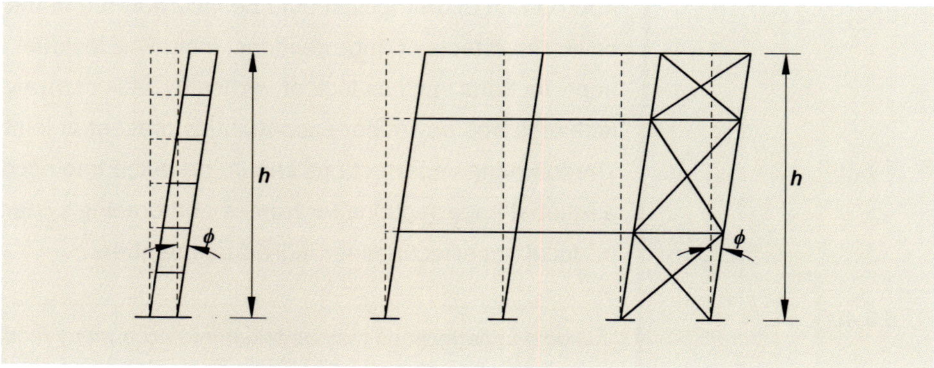

Figure 5.1 Equivalent sway imperfections

5.3.2(4)B

4. Sway imperfections may be disregarded where:

$H_{Ed} \geq 0.15\,V_{Ed}$

Satisfying this requirement would demand a relatively high horizontal load (generally due to the wind). In combinations of actions with gravity loads only, H_{Ed} is the equivalent horizontal force, which will be $0.005\,V_{Ed}$, or smaller, so in gravity only cases it will not be possible to satisfy this requirement.

In combinations that include wind loads, it is possible that $H_{Ed} > 0.15\,V_{Ed}$, in which case imperfections need not be allowed for.

5.3.2(5)B

5. For the determination of horizontal forces to floor diaphragms the configuration of imperfections as given in Figure 5.2 should be applied, where ϕ is a sway imperfection obtained from (3) assuming a single storey with height h, see (3) a).

The connection between the column and the floor diaphragm must be capable of carrying the force shown in Figure 5.2, which has a maximum value of $0.005\,N_{Ed}$. (It may be less, due to the α_h and α_m factors.)

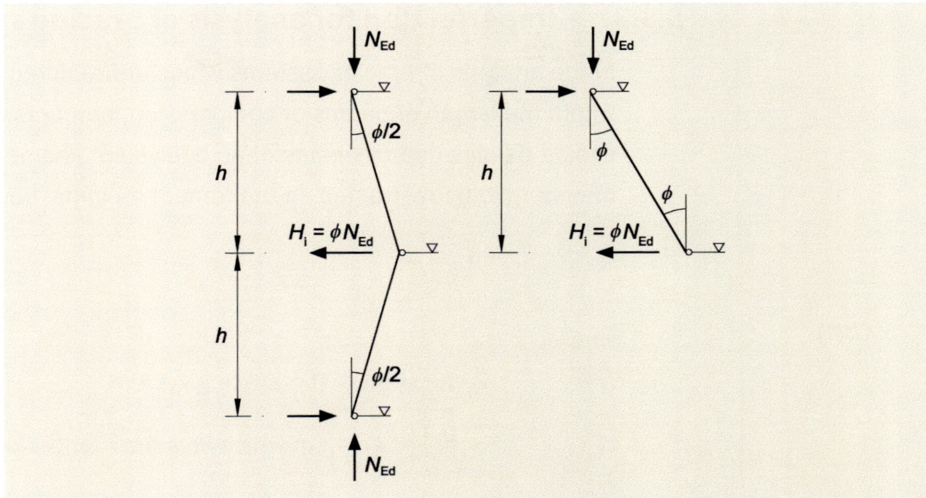

Figure 5.2 Configuration of sway imperfection Φ for horizontal forces on floor diaphragm

5.3.2(6) 6. When performing the global analysis for determining end forces and end moments to be used in member checks according to 6.3 local bow imperfections may be neglected.

Local bow imperfections must be modelled if the member is slender, and highly loaded in compression, and has a moment connection at least at one end of the member – see Clause 5.3.2 (6) of BS EN 1993-1-1. In orthodox cases, local bow imperfections are taken into account in the member checks.

5.3.2(7) 7. Figure 5.3 shows how the effects of initial sway imperfections may be replaced with equivalent horizontal forces, applied at the roof and floor levels.

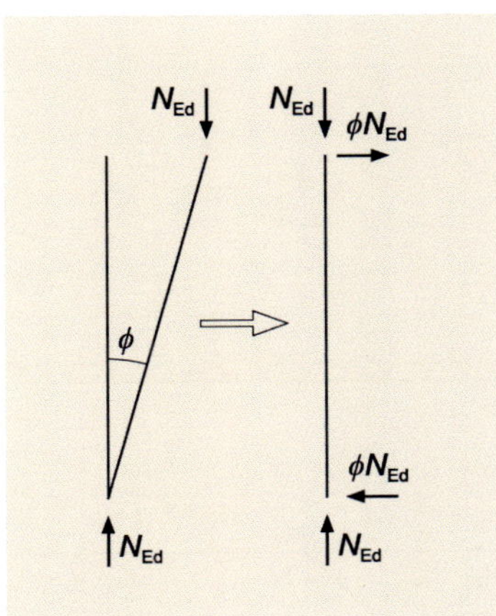

Figure 5.3 Replacement of initial imperfections by equivalent horizontal forces

5.3.2(8) 8. The initial sway imperfections should apply in all relevant horizontal directions, but need only be considered in one direction at a time.

5.3.2(9)B 9. Where, in multi-storey beam-and-column building frames, equivalent forces are used they should be applied at each floor and roof level.

5.3.2(10) 10. The possible torsional effects on a structure caused by anti-symmetric sways at the two opposite faces, should also be considered.

5.3.3 Imperfection for analysis of bracing systems

1. In the analysis of bracing systems which are required to provide lateral stability within the length of beams or compression members, the effects of imperfections should be included by means of an equivalent geometric imperfection of the members to be restrained, in the form of an initial bow imperfection.

$$e_0 = \alpha_m L/500$$

5.3.3(1)

where:

L is the span of the bracing system

α_m $= \sqrt{0.5\left(1+\frac{1}{m}\right)}$ in which m is the number of members to be restrained.

2. For convenience, the effects of the initial bow imperfections of the members to be restrained by a bracing system may be replaced by the equivalent stabilising force as shown in Figure 5.4.

$$q_d = \sum N_{Ed}\, 8\,\frac{e_0 + \delta_q}{L^2}$$

5.3.3(2)

where:

δ_q is the in-plane deflection of the bracing system due to q plus any external loads calculated from first order analysis

The use of the equivalent stabilising forces is recommended.

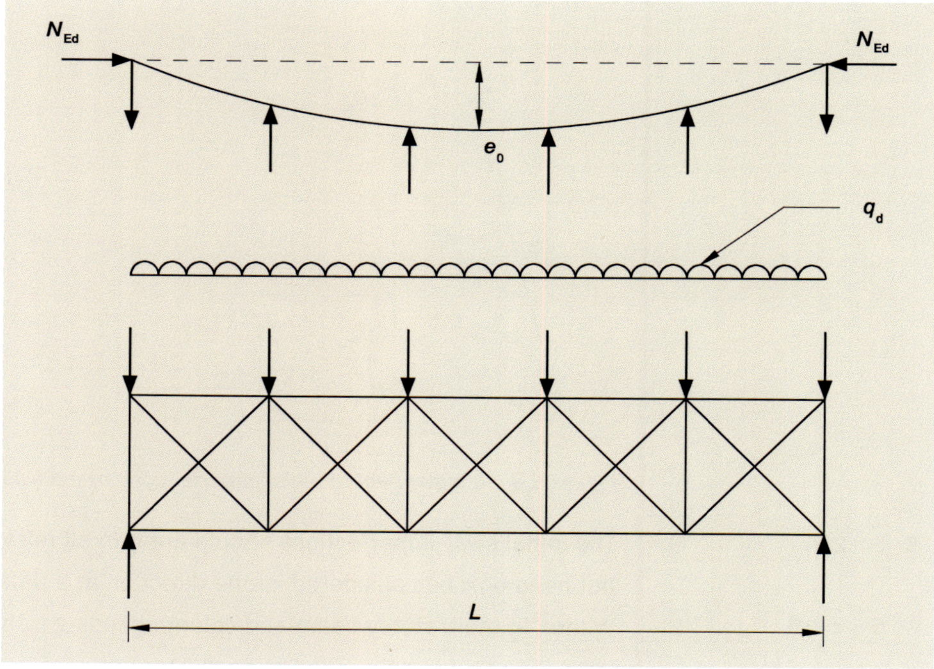

Figure 5.4 Equivalent stabilising force

5.3.3(4) 3. At points where beams or compression members are spliced, it should also be verified that the bracing system is able to resist a local force equal to $\alpha_m N_{Ed}/100$ applied to it by each beam or compression member which is spliced at that point, and to transmit this force to the adjacent points at which that beam or compression member is restrained.

5.3.3(5) 4. For checking the local force according to the preceding requirement, any external loads on the bracing system should also be included, but the forces arising from the imperfections in the bracing system may be omitted.

Clauses 5.3.3(3) and (4) above apply to the bracing members local to a splice. The lateral force of $\alpha_m N_{Ed}/100$ must be carried by the bracing members above and below the splice, in addition to the forces due to external loads. Each bracing system will generally have to carry the accumulated lateral force from several columns.

5.4 Methods of analysis

5.4.1 General

5.4.1(1) 1. Internal forces and moments should be determined using elastic global analysis.

EN 1993-1-1 allows the use of either elastic or plastic global analysis but the scope of this guide excludes plastic global analysis.

Guidance on the use of plastic analysis is given in BS EN 1993-1-1, Clause 5.4.3.

5.4.2 Elastic global analysis

5.4.2(1) 1. Elastic global analysis should be used on the assumption that the stress-strain behaviour of the material is linear, whatever the stress level is.

5.4.2(2) 2. Internal forces and moments may be calculated according to elastic global analysis even if the resistance of a cross section is based on its plastic resistance.

5.5 Classification of cross-sections

Section classification is given in resistance tables, such as the 'Blue Book' (*Steel building design: Design data,* SCI publication P363) and the 'Orange Book' (http://orangebook.arcelormittal.com). Tables for sections under combined axial load and bending include precalculated 'n limits' to facilitate classification of elements that are only part subject to compression.

5.5.2(1) 1. Four classes of cross-sections are defined, as follows:

- **Class 1** cross-sections are those which can form a plastic hinge with the rotation capacity required for plastic analysis without reduction of the resistance.

- **Class 2** cross-sections are those which can develop their plastic moment resistance, but which have limited rotation capacity because of local buckling.
- **Class 3** cross-sections are those in which the stress in the extreme compression fibre of the steel member assuming an elastic distribution of stresses can reach the yield strength, but local buckling is liable to prevent development of the plastic moment resistance.
- **Class 4** cross-sections are those in which local buckling will occur before the attainment of yield stress in one or more parts of the cross-section.

5.5.2(4)

2. Compression parts include every part of a cross-section which is either totally or partially in compression under the load combination considered.

5.5.2(6)

3. A cross-section is classified according to the highest (least favourable) class of its compression parts.

5.5.2(8)

4. The limiting proportions for Class 1, 2, and 3 compression parts should be obtained from Table 5.1 below.

5.5.2(8)

5. A part which fails to satisfy the limits for Class 3 should be taken as Class 4.

> Class 4 cross-sections are outside the scope of this guide.
>
> For outstands subject to transverse bending, the limiting values for uniform compression (Table 5.1 sheet 2) may be used conservatively.

Table 5.1 (Sheet 1 of 2): Maximum c/t ratios for compression parts

Internal compression parts

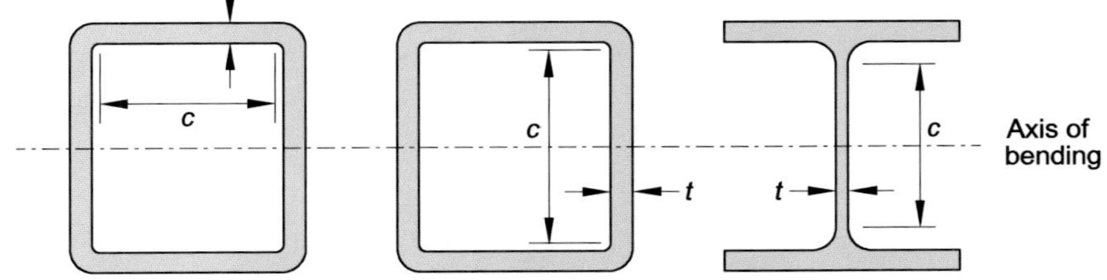

Class	Part subject to bending	Part subject to compression	Part subject to bending and compression	
Stress distribution in parts (compression positive)	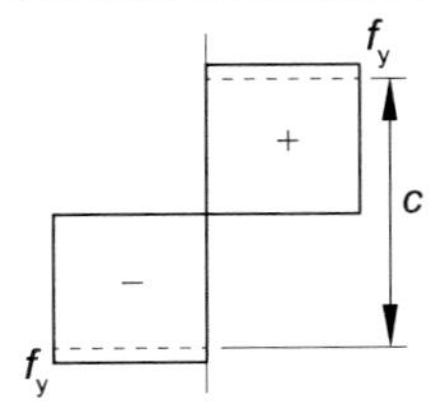	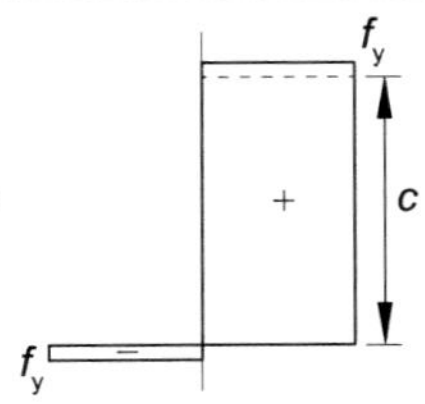	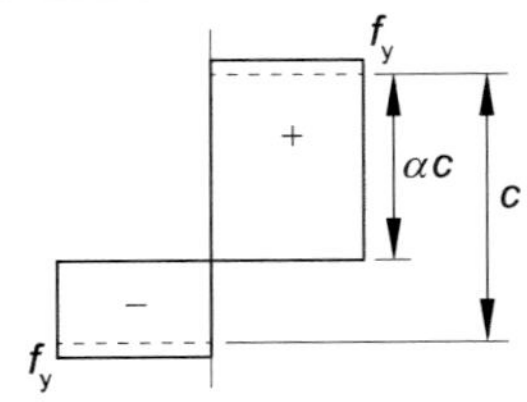	
1	$c/t \leq 72\varepsilon$	$c/t \leq 33\varepsilon$	when $\alpha > 0.5$	$\dfrac{396\varepsilon}{13\alpha - 1}$
			when $\alpha > 0.5$	$\dfrac{36\,\varepsilon}{\alpha}$
2	$c/t \leq 83\varepsilon$	$c/t \leq 38\varepsilon$	when $\alpha \leq 0.5$	$\dfrac{456\varepsilon}{13\alpha - 1}$
			when $\alpha \leq 0.5$	$\dfrac{41.5\varepsilon}{\alpha}$
	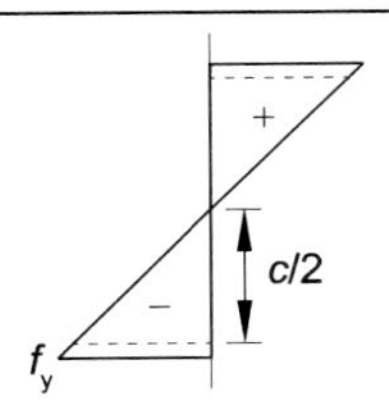	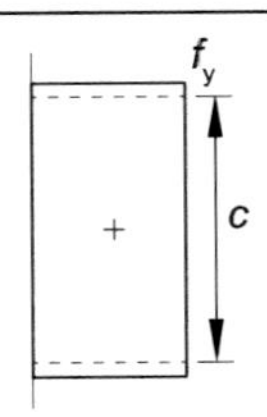	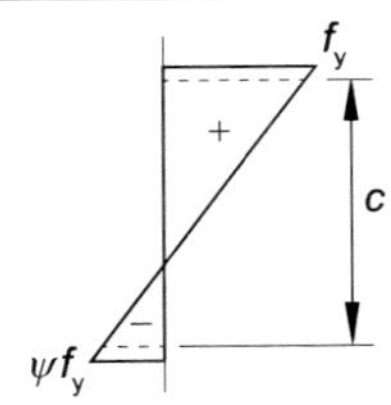	
3	$c/t \leq 124\varepsilon$	$c/t \leq 42\varepsilon$	when $\psi > -1$	$c/t \leq \dfrac{42\varepsilon}{0.67 + 0.33\psi}$
			when $\psi \leq -1$	$c/t \leq 62\varepsilon(1-\psi)\sqrt{(-\psi)}$

The values of ε, α and ψ are given by:

$$\varepsilon = \sqrt{235 / f_y}$$

$$\alpha = \frac{1}{2}\left(1 + \frac{N_{Ed}}{f_y\, c\, t_w}\right) \leq 1.0$$

$$\psi = \frac{2N_{Ed}}{Af_y} - 1$$

where N_{Ed} is positive in compression

Table 5.1 (Sheet 2 of 2): Maximum c/t ratios for compression parts

Outstand flanges

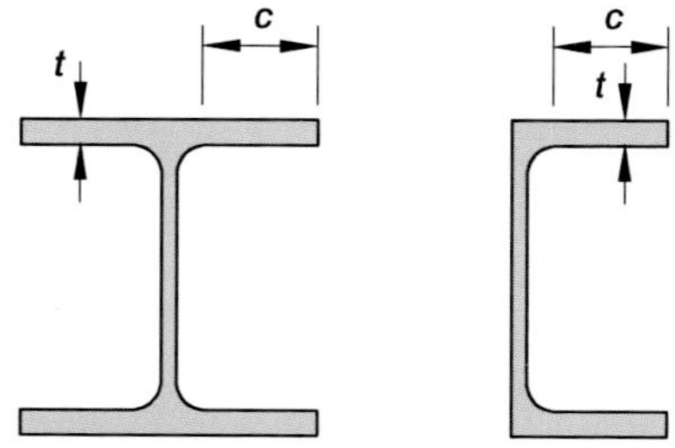

Rolled sections

Class	Part subject to compression
Stress distribution in parts (compression positive)	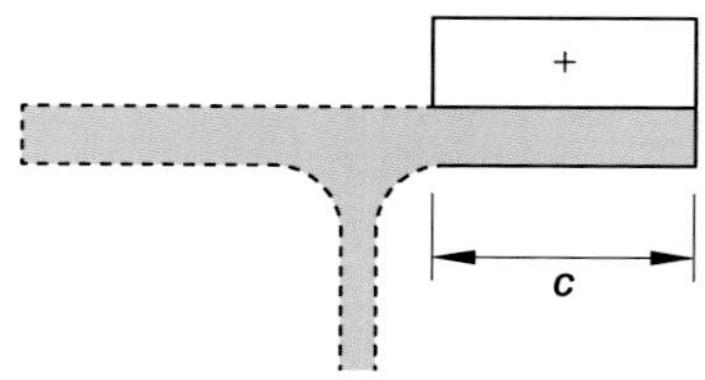
1	$c/t \leq 9\varepsilon$
2	$c/t \leq 10\varepsilon$
3	$c/t \leq 14\varepsilon$

Angles

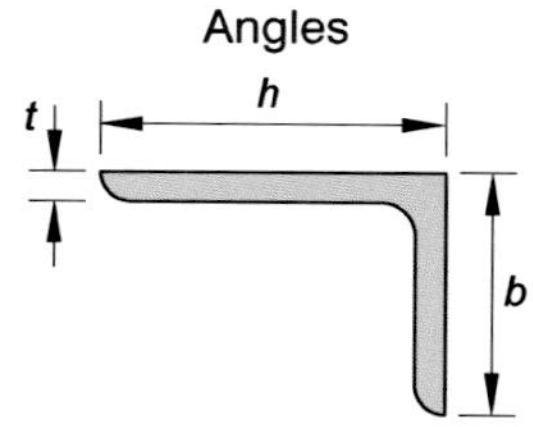

Class	Section in compression
Stress distribution across section (compression positive)	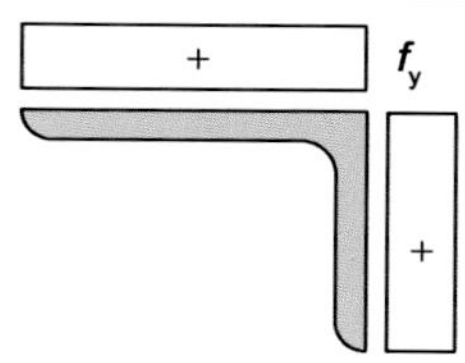
3	$h/t \leq 15\varepsilon$ $\quad \dfrac{b+h}{2t} \leq 11.5\varepsilon$

Tubular sections

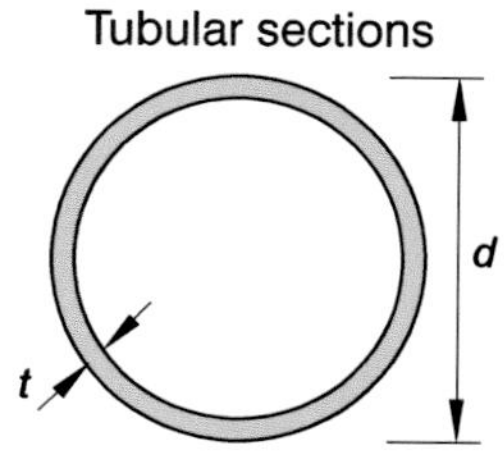

Class	Section in bending and/or compression
1	$d/t \leq 50\varepsilon^2$
2	$d/t \leq 70\varepsilon^2$
3	$d/t \leq 90\varepsilon^2$

$\varepsilon = \sqrt{235 / f_y}$

ULTIMATE LIMIT STATES

6.1 Partial factors for resistance

6.1(1)

1. The partial factors γ_M should be applied to the various characteristic values of resistance in this section as follows:

NA.2.15

- Resistance of cross-section whatever the class is: $\gamma_{M0} = 1.00$
- Resistance of members to instability: $\gamma_{M1} = 1.00$
- Resistance of cross-sections in tension to fracture: $\gamma_{M2} = 1.10$

γ_{M2} is used with ultimate material strengths, for example when verifying net areas subject to tension (see 6.2.3(3)(b)) and when verifying net areas subject to shear in connection design. A different value of γ_{M2} is used when calculating the resistance of connection components.

For the partial factors for resistance of joints, see Section 2.5.1.

6.2 Resistance of cross-sections

6.2.1 General

6.2.1(1)

1. The design value of an action effect in each cross-section should not exceed the corresponding resistance and if several action effects act simultaneously, the combined effect should not exceed the resistance for that combination.

6.2.1(7)

2. As a conservative approximation for all cross-sections, a linear summation of the utilisation ratios for each resistance may be used. For the combination of N_{Ed}, $M_{y,Ed}$ and $M_{z,Ed}$ this method may be applied using the following criteria:

$$\frac{N_{Ed}}{N_{Rd}} + \frac{M_{y,Ed}}{M_{y,Rd}} + \frac{M_{z,Ed}}{M_{z,Rd}} \leq 1$$

Where N_{Rd}, $M_{y,Rd}$ and $M_{z,Rd}$ are the design values of the resistance depending on the cross-sectional classification and including any reduction that might be caused by shear effects (see 6.2.7).

6.2.2 Section properties

6.2.2.1 *Gross cross-section*

6.2.2.1(1) 1. The properties of the gross cross-section should be determined using the nominal dimensions. Holes for fasteners need not be deducted, but allowance should be made for larger openings. Splice materials should not be included.

6.2.2.2 *Net sections*

6.2.2.2(1) 1. The net area of a cross-section should be taken as its gross area less appropriate deductions for all holes and other openings.

6.2.2.2(2) 2. For calculating net section properties, the deduction for a single fastener hole should be the gross cross-sectional area of the hole in the plane of its axis. For countersunk holes, appropriate allowance should be made for the countersunk portion.

> For deductions where the holes are staggered, refer to BS EN 1993-1-1 Clause 6.2.2.2(4).

6.2.3 Tension

6.2.3(1) 1. The design value of the tension force N_{Ed} at each cross-section should satisfy:

(6.5)
$$\frac{N_{Ed}}{N_{t,Rd}} \leq 1.0$$

6.2.3(2) 2. For sections without holes, the design tension resistance $N_{t,Rd}$ should be taken as the design plastic resistance of the gross cross-section:

(6.6)
$$N_{pl,Rd} = \frac{Af_y}{\gamma_{M0}}$$

6.2.3(2) 3. For sections with holes, the design tension resistance $N_{t,Rd}$ should be taken as the smaller of:

- The plastic resistance of the gross cross-section (given above); and
- The design ultimate resistance of the net cross-section at holes for fasteners:

(6.7)
$$N_{u,Rd} = \frac{0.9A_{net}f_u}{\gamma_{M2}}$$

6.2.3(5) 4. For angles connected through one leg, see BS EN 1993-1-8 Clause 3.10.3. Similar consideration should also be given to other types of sections connected through outstands.

6.2.4 Compression

6.2.4(1) 1. The design value of the compression force N_{Ed} at each cross-section should satisfy:

(6.9)
$$\frac{N_{Ed}}{N_{c,Rd}} \leq 1.0$$

6.2.4(2) — 2. The design resistance of the cross-section for uniform compression $N_{c,Rd}$ should be determined as follows:

(6.10)

$$N_{c,Rd} = \frac{Af_y}{\gamma_{M0}} \quad \text{for class 1, 2 or 3 cross-sections}$$

6.2.4(3) — 3. Fastener holes, except for oversize and slotted holes as defined in EN 1090, need not be allowed for in compression members, provided that they are filled by fasteners.

> For members of uniform cross-sections in axial compression the design buckling resistance, $N_{b,Rd}$ (see Section 6.3.1) always governs unless oversized or slotted holes are used.

6.2.5 Bending

6.2.5(1) — 1. The design value of the bending moment M_{Ed} at each cross-section should satisfy:

(6.12)

$$\frac{M_{Ed}}{M_{c,Rd}} \leq 1,0$$

where:

$M_{c,Rd}$ is determined considering fastener holes, see (3) to (5).

6.2.5(2) — 2. The design resistance for bending about one principal axis of a cross-section is determined as follows:

(6.13)

$$M_{c,Rd} = M_{pl,Rd} = \frac{W_{pl} f_y}{\gamma_{M0}} \quad \text{for Class 1 or 2 cross-sections}$$

(6.14)

$$M_{c,Rd} = M_{el,Rd} = \frac{W_{el,min} f_y}{\gamma_{M0}} \quad \text{for Class 3 cross-sections}$$

where:

$W_{el,min}$ corresponds to the fibre with the maximum elastic stress.

> For bending about both axes, the following criterion may be used for I and H sections.
>
> $$\left[\frac{M_{y,Ed}}{M_{N,y,Rd}}\right]^2 + \left[\frac{M_{z,Ed}}{M_{N,z,Rd}}\right] \leq 1$$
>
> This criterion is derived from that in BS EN 1993-1-1, 6.2.8.1(6) for $N_{Ed} = 0$.

6.2.5(4) — 3. Fastener holes in the tension flange may be ignored in determining the bending resistance provided that for the tension flange:

(6.16)

$$\frac{A_{f,net} 0.9 f_u}{\gamma_{M2}} \geq \frac{A_f f_y}{\gamma_{M0}}$$

where:

A_f is the area of the tension flange.

6.2.5(5) 4. Fastener holes in the tension zone of the web need not be allowed for, provided that the limit given in (3) is satisfied for the complete tension zone comprising the tension flange plus the tension zone of the web.

6.2.5(6) 5. Fastener holes, except for oversize and slotted holes, in the compression zone of the cross-section need not be allowed for, provided they are filled by fasteners.

6.2.6 Shear

6.2.6(1) 1. The design value of the shear force V_{Ed} at each cross-section should satisfy:

(6.17)

$$\frac{V_{Ed}}{V_{c,Rd}} \leq 1.0$$

where:

$V_{c,Rd}$ is the design plastic shear resistance $V_{pl,Rd}$.

6.2.6(2) 2. In the absence of torsion, the design plastic shear resistance is given by:

(6.18)

$$V_{pl,Rd} = \frac{A_v\left(f_y / \sqrt{3}\right)}{\gamma_{M0}}$$

where:

A_v is the shear area.

Torsional effects are outside the scope of this guide

6.2.6(3) 3. The shear area A_v may be taken as follows:

a. Rolled I and H sections, load parallel to web: $A - 2bt_f + (t_w + 2r)t_f$

Rolled channel sections, load parallel to web: $A - 2bt_f + (t_w + r)t_f$

b. Rolled T-sections, load parallel to web: $A_v = A - bt_f + (t_w + 2r)t_f \frac{t_f}{2}$

c. Rolled rectangular hollow sections,

Load parallel to depth $Ah/(b + h)$

Load parallel to width $Ab/(b + h)$

Based on 6.2.6(6) 4. Shear buckling in webs without intermediate stiffeners is avoided if:

$$\frac{h_w}{t_w} \leq 72\frac{\varepsilon}{\eta}$$

It is conservative to assume a value of (the conversion factor) $\eta = 1$. η is considered in BS EN 1993-1-5.

6.2.6(7) 5. Fastener holes need not be allowed for in shear verification except in verifying the design shear resistance at connection zones as given in BS EN 1991-1-8.

A deduction for fastener holes is made when checking block tearing in accordance with BS EN 1991-1-8 Clause 3.10.2 (See Section 8.2.9 of this guide).

6.2.7 Bending and shear

↖ 6.2.8(1) 1. Where shear is present, allowance should be made for its effect on bending resistance.

↖ 6.2.8(2) 2. Where $V_{Ed} < 0.5V_{pl,Rd}$ (see 6.2.6(2)) the effect of the shear force on the bending resistance may be neglected, except where shear buckling reduces the section resistance.

↖ 6.2.8(3) 3. Where $V_{Ed} \geq 0.5V_{pl,Rd}$ the reduced moment resistance should be taken as the design resistance of the cross-section, calculated using a reduced yield strength:

↖ (6.29) $(1-\rho)f_y$ for the shear area,

where:

$$\rho = \left(\frac{2V_{Ed}}{V_{pl,Rd}} - 1\right)^2$$

and $V_{pl,Rd}$ is obtained from 6.2.6(2)

↖ Note to 6.2.10(3) 4. Instead of reducing the yield strength, the plate thickness of the relevant part of the cross-section may be reduced.

For verification of Class 3 sections, reducing the web plate thickness often results in a smaller reduction in bending resistance than limiting the resistance to that corresponding to the reduced web strength (when the resistance is limited by the stress at the web/flange junction).

↖ 6.2.8(5) 5. The reduced plastic section resistance moment allowing for the shear force may be obtained for I cross-sections with equal flanges and bending about the major axis as follows

↖ (6.30)

$$M_{v,y,Rd} = \frac{\left[W_{pl,y} - \frac{\rho A_w^2}{4t_w}\right] f_y}{\gamma_{M0}}$$

↖ 6.2.8(6) but $M_{v,y,Rd} \leq M_{c,y,Rd}$

where:

$M_{c,y,Rd}$ is obtained from 6.2.5(2)

A_w $= h_w t_w$

6.2.9

6.2.8 Bending and axial force

6.2.8.1 Class 1 and 2 cross-sections

6.2.9.1(2)

6.2.1(2) allows a simple interaction criterion to be used for bending (uniaxial or biaxial) with axial force. The following rules give a more detailed and less conservative verification for Class 1 and Class 2 cross-sections. For situations where shear is also present, see 6.2.9.

6.2.9.1(1)

1. When an axial force is present allowance should be made for its effect on the plastic moment resistance.

6.2.9.1(2)

2. For Class 1 and 2 cross-sections, the following criteria should be satisfied:

$$M_{Ed} \leq M_{N,Rd}$$

where:

(6.31)

$M_{N,Rd}$ is the design plastic moment resistance reduced due to the axial force N_{Ed}.

6.2.9.1(4)

3. For doubly symmetric I- and H-sections or other flanged sections, allowance need not be made for the effect of the axial force on the plastic resistance moment about the y-y axis when both the following are satisfied:

(6.33)

$N_{Ed} \leq 0.25 N_{pl,Rd}$ and

(6.34)

$$N_{Ed} \leq \frac{0.5\, h_w\, t_w\, f_y}{\gamma_{M0}}$$

6.2.9.1(4)

4. For doubly symmetrical I- and H- sections, allowance need not be made for the effect of the axial force on the plastic resistance moment about the z-z axis when:

(6.35)

$$N_{Ed} \leq \frac{h_w\, t_w\, f_y}{\gamma_{M0}}$$

6.2.9.1(5)

5. The following approximations may be used for standard rolled I or H sections and for welded I or H sections with equal flanges:

(6.36)

$M_{N,y,Rd} = M_{pl,y,Rd}\,(1 - n)/(1 - 0.5a)$ but $M_{N,y,Rd} \leq M_{pl,yRd}$

(6.37)

for $n \leq a$: $M_{N,z,Rd} = M_{pl,z,Rd}$

(6.38)

for $n > a$: $M_{N,z,Rd} = M_{pl,z,Rd}\left[1 - \left(\frac{n - a}{1 - a}\right)^2\right]$

where:

n $= N_{Ed}/N_{pl,Rd}$

a $= (A - 2bt_f)/A$ but $a \leq 0.5$

For rectangular structural hollow sections:

(6.39) $$M_{N,y,Rd} = M_{pl,y,Rd}(1-n)/(1-0.5a_w) \quad \text{but } M_{N,y,Rd} \le M_{pl,yRd}$$

(6.40) $$M_{N,z,Rd} = M_{pl,z,Rd}(1-n)/(1-0.5a_f) \quad \text{but } M_{N,z,Rd} \le M_{pl,z,Rd}$$

where:

$a_w = (A - 2bt)/A$ but $a_w \le 0.5$

$a_f = (A - 2ht)/A$ but $a_f \le 0.5$

6.2.9.1(6)

6. For biaxial bending, the following criterion may be used:

(6.41) $$\left[\frac{M_{y,Ed}}{M_{N,y,Rd}}\right]^{\alpha} + \left[\frac{M_{z,Ed}}{M_{N,z,Rd}}\right]^{\beta} \le 1$$

In which α and β are constants, which for I and H sections may be taken as follows:

$\alpha = 2;\ \beta = 5n$ but $\beta \ge 1$

where:

$n = N_{Ed}/N_{pl,Rd}$

6.2.8.2 *Class 3 cross-sections*

6.2.9.2(1)

1. For Class 3 cross-sections the maximum longitudinal stress due to moment and axial force, taking account of fastener holes where relevant (see 6.2.3, 6.2.4 and 6.2.5) should not exceed f_y/γ_{M0}.

> This criterion is effectively the same as that in 6.2.1(2).

6.2.9 Bending, shear and axial force

6.2.10(2)

1. Where $V_{Ed} \le 0.5\,V_{pl,Rd}$, no reduction of the resistances defined for bending and axial force in 6.2.8 need be made.

6.2.10(3)

2. Where $V_{Ed} > 0.5\,V_{pl,Rd}$, the design resistance of the cross-section to combinations of moment and axial force should be calculated using a reduced yield strength, as given by 6.2.7(3).

6.3 Buckling resistance of members

6.3.1 Uniform members in compression

BS EN 1993-1-1 covers three modes of buckling when subject to axial compression:

flexural buckling (commonly known as strut buckling).

torsional buckling which may be critical for cruciform sections subject to axial compression.

torsional-flexural buckling which may be critical for asymmetric sections subject to axial compression.

Torsional buckling and torsional flexural buckling are not the critical buckling modes for doubly symmetric I or H sections or hollow sections.

6.3.1.1 Buckling resistance

6.3.1.1(1)

1. A compression member should be verified against buckling as follows:

(6.46)

$$\frac{N_{Ed}}{N_{b,Rd}} \leq 1.0$$

where:

N_{Ed} is the design value of the compression force

$N_{b,Rd}$ is the design buckling resistance of the compression member

6.3.1.1(3)

2. The design buckling resistance of a compression member should be taken as:

(6.47)

$$N_{b,Rd} = \chi \frac{A f_y}{\gamma_{M1}}$$ for Class 1, 2 and 3 cross-sections

where:

χ is the reduction factor for the relevant buckling mode

6.3.1.2 Buckling curves

6.3.1.2(1)

1. For axial compression in members, the value of χ for the appropriate non-dimensional slenderness $\bar{\lambda}$ may be determined from the appropriate buckling curve according to:

(6.49)

$$\chi = \frac{1}{\varphi + \sqrt{\varphi^2 - \bar{\lambda}^2}}$$ but $\chi \leq 1$

where:

φ $= 0.5\left[1 + \alpha\left(\bar{\lambda} - 0.2\right) + \bar{\lambda}^2\right]$

α is an imperfection factor

2. The non-dimensional slenderness $\bar{\lambda}$ is given by:

$$\bar{\lambda} = \sqrt{\frac{Af_y}{N_{cr}}}$$

where:

N_{cr} is the elastic critical force for the relevant buckling mode

> For each mode of buckling, the value of N_{cr} should be determined, and the lowest value of $\bar{\lambda}$ used.
>
> For open sections (UB, UC), the torsional and torsional-flexural buckling modes are not critical. For angles an effective slenderness ratio should be calculated from Annex BB.1.2 of BS EN 1993-1-1. A similar effective slenderness should be calculated for channels which are only connected through the web.
>
> For flexural, or strut buckling, N_{cr} is the Euler load, i.e. $N_{cr} = \frac{\pi^2 EI}{L^2}$

6.3.1.3(1)

3. For flexural buckling only, $\bar{\lambda}$ is given by:

(6.50)

$$\bar{\lambda} = \sqrt{\frac{Af_y}{N_{cr}}} = \frac{L_{cr}}{i}\frac{1}{\lambda_1}$$ for Class 1, 2 and 3 cross-sections

where:

L_{cr} is the buckling length in the buckling plane considered

i is the radius of gyration about the relevant axis, determined using the properties of the gross cross-section

λ_1 = 86 for grade S275

= 76 for grade S355

= 70 for grade S420

= 67 for grade S460

> The above values of λ_1 are based on the ε parameter for material up to 16 mm thick. It is conservative to use the values for sections with thicker elements.

4. The imperfection factor α corresponding to the appropriate buckling curve should be obtained from Table 6.1 based on the selection from Table 6.2.

> The value of χ for the appropriate non-dimensional slenderness $\bar{\lambda}$ may alternatively be determined from Figure 6.1 or Table 6.3.
>
> Figure 6.1 and Table 6.3 are based on the expression for χ and offer simpler determination than evaluation of the formulae.

Table 6.1 Imperfection factors for flexural buckling curves

Buckling Curve	a_0	a	b	c	d
Imperfection factor α	0.13	0.21	0.34	0.49	0.76

Table 6.2 Selection of flexural buckling curve for a cross-section

	Cross-section		**Limits**	**Buckling about axis**	**Buckling Curve** S275 S355 S420	**Buckling Curve** S460
Rolled sections	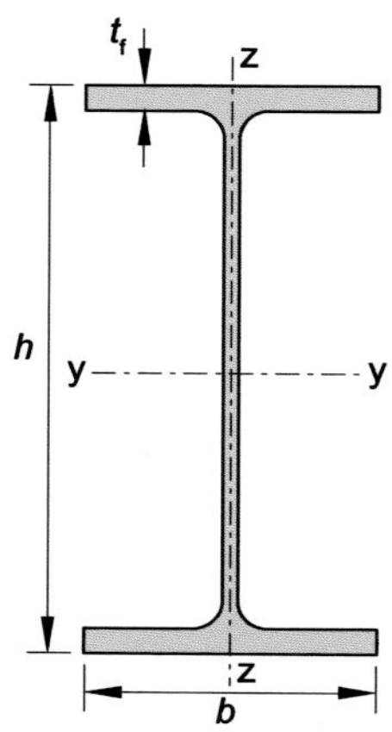	$h/b > 1.2$	$t_f \leq 40$ mm	y–y	a	a_0
				z–z	b	a_0
		$h/b > 1.2$	40 mm $< t_f \leq 100$	y–y	b	a
				z–z	c	a
		$h/b \leq 1.2$	$t_f \leq 100$ mm	y–y	b	a
				z–z	c	a
		$h/b \leq 1.2$	$t_f > 100$ mm	y–y	d	c
				z–z	d	c
U-, T- and solid sections	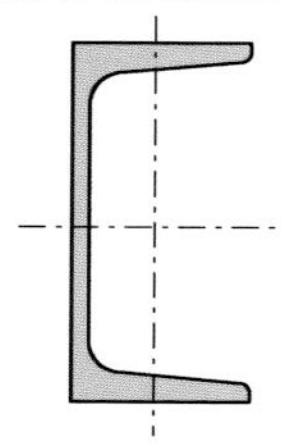			any	c	c
L-sections	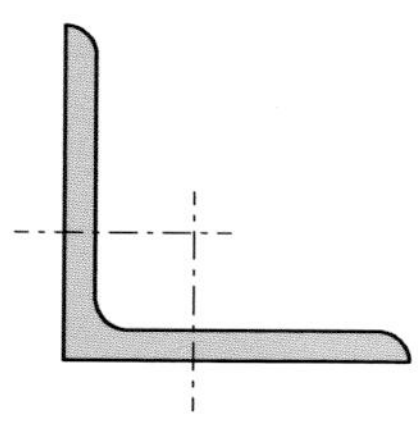			any	b	b
Hollow sections	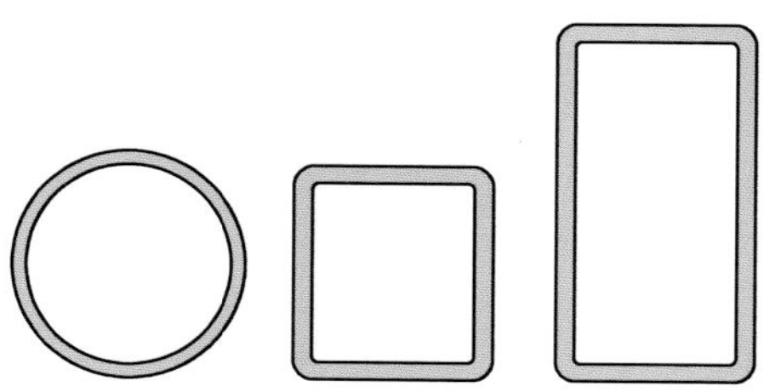		hot finished	any	a	a_0
			cold formed	any	c	c

Figure 6.1 *Buckling curves*

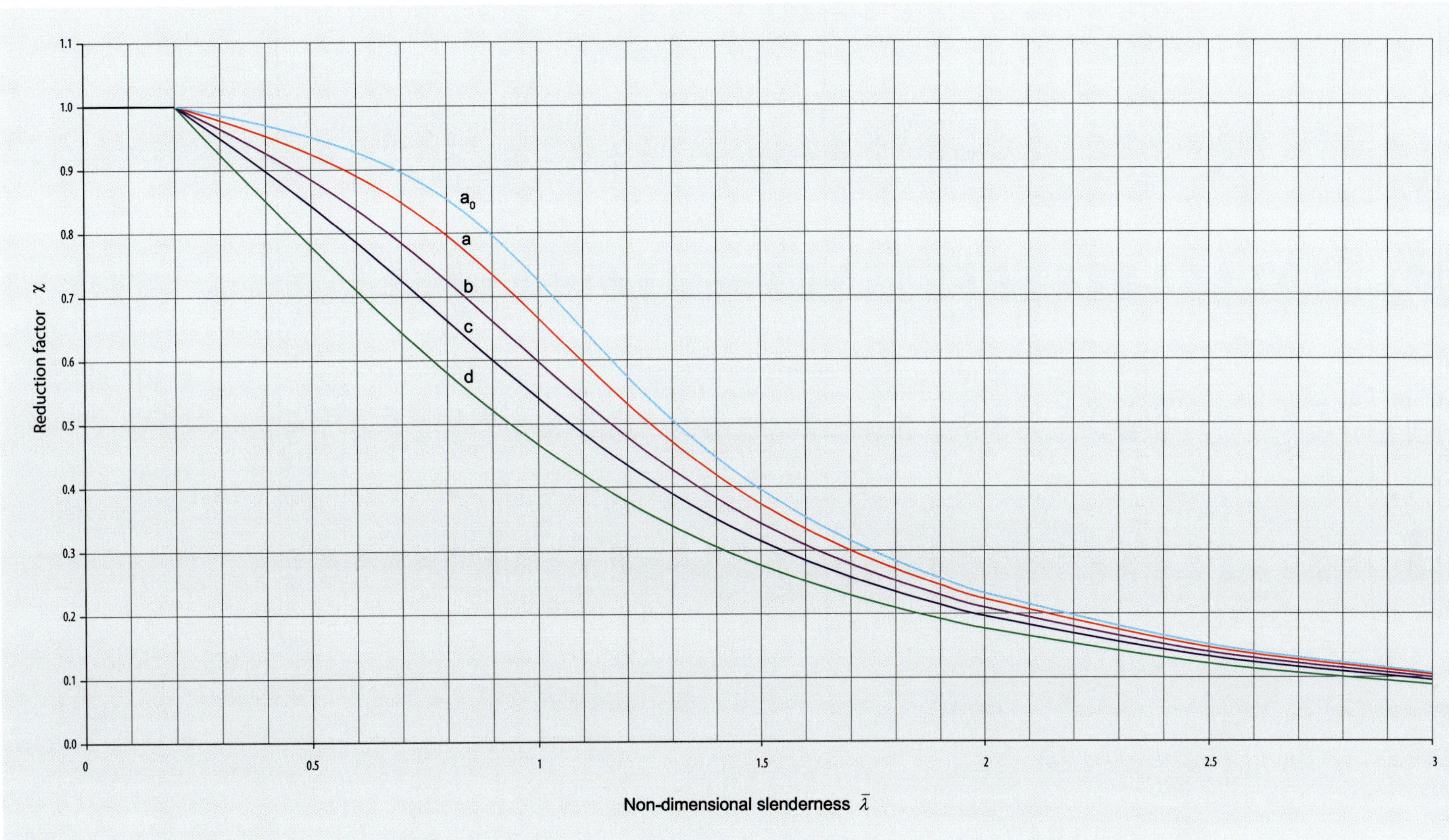

Table 6.3 Flexural buckling reduction factor, χ

$\bar{\lambda}$	Buckling curve				
	a_0	a	b	c	d
0.20	1.00	1.00	1.00	1.00	1.00
0.25	0.99	0.99	0.98	0.97	0.96
0.30	0.99	0.98	0.96	0.95	0.92
0.35	0.98	0.97	0.95	0.92	0.89
0.40	0.97	0.95	0.93	0.90	0.85
0.45	0/96	0.94	0.91	0.87	0.81
0.50	0.95	0.92	0.88	0.84	0.78
0.55	0.94	0.91	0.86	0.81	0.74
0.60	0.93	0.89	0.84	0.79	0.71
0.65	0.91	0.87	0.81	0.76	0.68
0.70	0.90	0.85	0.78	0.72	0.64
0.75	0.88	0.82	0.75	0.69	0.61
0.80	0.85	0.80	0.72	0.66	0.58
0.85	0.83	0.77	0.69	0.63	0.55
0.90	0.80	0.73	0.66	0.60	0.52
0.95	0.76	0.70	0.63	0.57	0.49
1.00	0.73	0.67	0.60	0.54	0.47
1.05	0.69	0.63	0.57	0.51	0.44
1.10	0.65	0.60	0.54	0.48	0.42
1.15	0.61	0.56	0.51	0.46	0.40
1.20	0.57	0.53	0.48	0.43	0.38
1.25	0.54	0.50	0.45	0.41	0.36
1.30	0.51	0.47	0.43	0.39	0.34
1.35	0.47	0.44	0.40	0.37	0.32
1.40	0.45	0.42	0.38	0.35	0.31
1.45	0.42	0.39	0.36	0.33	0.29
1.50	0.40	0.37	0.34	0.31	0.28
1.60	0.35	0.33	0.31	0.28	0.25
1.70	0.31	0.30	0.28	0.26	0.23
1.80	0.28	0.27	0.25	0.23	0.21
1.90	0.26	0.24	0.23	0.21	0.19
2.00	0.23	0.22	0.21	0.20	0.18
2.50	0.15	0.15	0.14	0.13	0.12
3.00	0.11	0.10	0.10	0.10	0.09

6.3.2 Uniform members in bending

6.3.2.1 Resistance

6.3.2.1(1)

1. A laterally unrestrained member subject to major axis bending should be verified against lateral-torsional buckling as follows:

(6.54)

$$\frac{M_{Ed}}{M_{b,Rd}} \leq 1.0$$

where:

M_{Ed} is the design value of the moment

$M_{b,Rd}$ is the design buckling resistance moment.

6.3.2.1(2)

2. Beams with sufficient restraint to the compression flange are not susceptible to lateral torsional buckling.

6.3.2.1(3)

3. The design buckling resistance of a laterally unrestrained beam should be taken as:

$$M_{b,Rd} = \chi_{LT} W_y \frac{f_y}{\gamma_{M1}}$$

(6.55)

where:

W_y is the appropriate section modulus as follows:

$W_y = W_{pl,y}$ for Class 1 and 2 cross-sections

$W_y = W_{el,y}$ for Class 3 cross-sections

χ_{LT} is the reduction factor for lateral-torsional buckling.

6.3.2.2 Lateral torsional buckling curves - general case

Note: ***The rules for "Lateral torsional buckling curves - general case" are not included in this guide because the scope of the guide is limited to the use of rolled sections, for which slightly different buckling curves apply. Refer to BS EN 1993-1-1 Clause 6.3.2.2 and the National Annex if welded sections are to be used.***

6.3.2.3 *Lateral torsional buckling curves for rolled sections*

Note: *The Standard treats "equivalent welded sections" in the same way as rolled sections, but the NA requires the use of a modified approach.*

6.3.2.3 and NA.2.17

1. For rolled sections of constant cross-section in bending, the value of χ_{LT} for the appropriate non-dimensional slenderness $\bar{\lambda}_{LT}$ should be determined from:

$$\chi_{LT} = \frac{1}{\phi_{LT} + \sqrt{\phi_{LT}^2 - \beta\bar{\lambda}_{LT}^2}} \qquad \text{but } \chi_{LT} \le 1$$

where:

$\phi_{LT} = 0.5\left[1 + \alpha_{LT}\left(\bar{\lambda}_{LT} - \bar{\lambda}_{LT,0}\right) + \beta\bar{\lambda}_{LT}^2\right]$

$\bar{\lambda}_{LT,0} = 0.4$ for rolled sections

$\beta = 0.75$ for rolled sections

$$\bar{\lambda}_{LT} = \sqrt{\frac{W_y f_y}{M_{cr}}}$$

where:

W_y is the appropriate section modulus for the section classification

M_{cr} is the elastic critical moment for lateral-torsional buckling

An expression to evaluate M_{cr} is not given in BS EN 1993-1-1. Three methods are given in this publication to assist in the determination of lateral-torsional buckling resistance.

Method 1

NCCI Document SN003 (available from www.steel-ncci.com) provides appropriate expressions to calculate M_{cr}. For loads which are not destabilising, and for doubly symmetric sections (i.e. UB and UC):

$$M_{cr} = C_1 \frac{\pi^2 EI_z}{L^2} \sqrt{\frac{I_w}{I_z} + \frac{L^2 GI_t}{\pi^2 EI_z}}$$

where:

E and G are material properties

I_z, I_t, I_w are section properties

L is the buckling length of the member

C_1 is a factor that depends on the shape of the bending moment diagram – see Table 6.4 of this publication.

Method 2

The value of M_{cr} may be determined using software, for example the M_{Cr} tool available at www.steelconstruction.info and '*LTBeamN*' available from www.cticm.com

Method 3

As a very conservative alternative to calculating M_{cr} and hence $\bar{\lambda}_{LT}$, the value of $\bar{\lambda}_{LT}$ may be calculated directly from the expression given below.

Where loads are not destabilising, for simply supported rolled I, H and channel sections, the non-dimensional slenderness $\bar{\lambda}_{LT}$ is given by:

$$\bar{\lambda}_{LT} = \frac{1}{\sqrt{C_1}} UV\bar{\lambda}_z\sqrt{\beta_w}$$

where:

$\frac{1}{\sqrt{C_1}}$ is a parameter dependant on the shape of the bending moment diagram, and which may conservatively be taken as 1.0, or otherwise given in Table 6.4 for loads which are not destabilising

U is a section property (given in section property tables, or may conservatively be taken as 0.9)

V is a parameter related to slenderness, and for symmetric rolled sections where the loads are not destabilising, may be conservatively taken as 1.0 or as:

$$V = \frac{1}{\sqrt[4]{1 + \frac{1}{20}\left(\frac{\lambda_z}{h/t_f}\right)^2}}$$

Conservatively, the product and U and V may be taken as 0.9

where:

λ_z $= \frac{kL}{i_z}$ in which k may conservatively be taken as 1.0 for beams supported and restrained against twist at both ends. With certain additional restraint conditions k may be less than 1.0, as described in Appendix F, Section F.1 For the value of k for cantilevers, see Section F.3

$\bar{\lambda}_z$ $= \frac{\lambda_z}{\lambda_1}$

L is the distance between points of lateral restraint

λ_1 may be taken as:

$= 86$	for Grade S275	$= 76$	for Grade S355
$= 70$	for Grade S420	$= 67$	for Grade S460

β_w $= \frac{W_y}{W_{pl,y}}$

It is conservative to assume that the product $UV = 0.9$ and that $\beta_w = 1.0$

In its most conservative form, $\bar{\lambda}_{LT} = \frac{L/i_z}{85}$ for S355

Method 3 is amenable to presentation in a tabular format whereby $\bar{\lambda}_{LT}$ may be calculated directly, based on the slenderness L/i_z and h/t_f. This is presented in Appendix E, with an example.

Methods 1 and 2 give similar results. In method 3, the assumptions that $C_1 = 1.0$ and that $UV = 0.9$ can be very conservative.

Where loads are destabilising, a parameter D should be introduced in the expression for $\bar{\lambda}_{LT}$, as shown in Appendix F Section F.1. The values of D are shown in Sections F.1 and F.3.

Table 6.4 Values of $\frac{1}{\sqrt{C_1}}$ and C1 for typical moment conditions (load is not destabilising)

End Moment Loading	ψ	$\frac{1}{\sqrt{C_1}}$	C_1
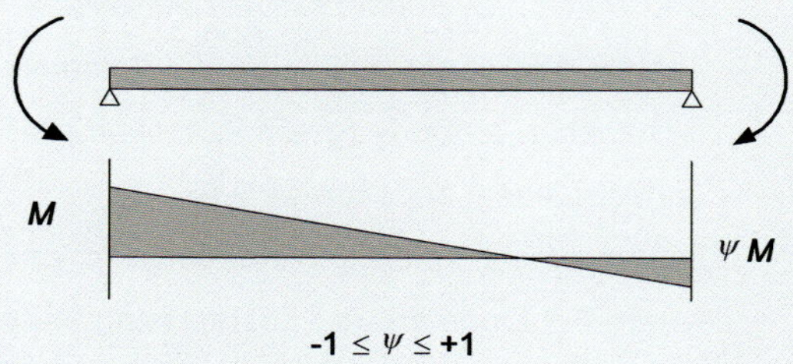	+1.00	1.00	1.00
	+0.75	0.92	1.17
	+0.50	0.86	1.36
	+0.25	0.80	1.56
	0.00	0.75	1.77
	-0.25	0.71	2.00
	-0.50	0.67	2.24
	-0.75	0.63	2.49
	-1.00	0.60	2.76
Intermediate Transverse Loading			
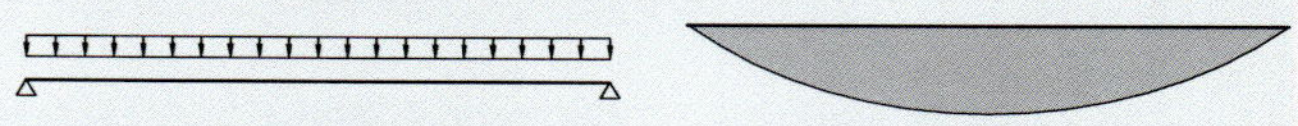		0.94	1.13
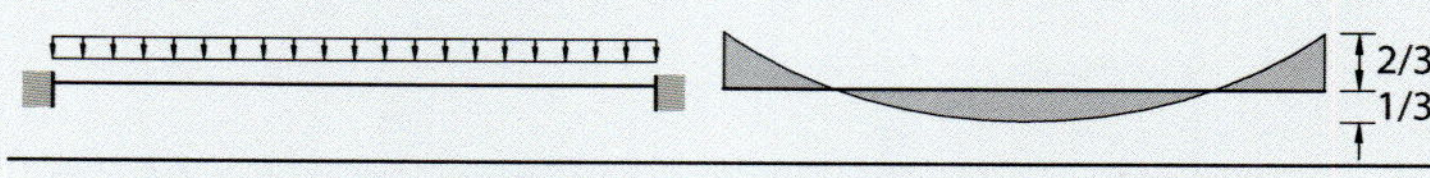		0.62	2.60*
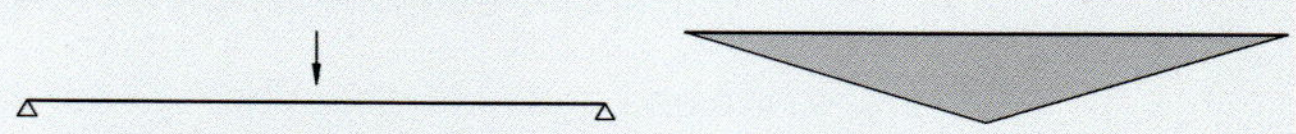		0.86	1.35
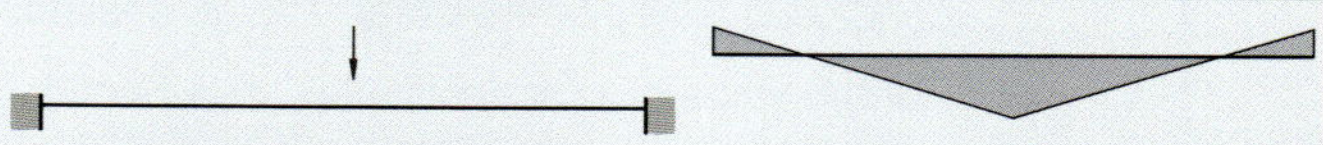		0.77	1.69

* This value is valid when the moment distribution is elastic (end moments are twice that at mid-span). For other distributions the value will differ (e.g. for equal moments at the ends and mid-span, which might be the case with a plastic distribution, $C_1 = 1.29$).

Note to 6.3.2.2(2), 6.3 and NA.2.16

2. The value of the imperfection parameter α_{LT} corresponding to the appropriate buckling curve is given by Table 6.5 below.

Table 6.5 Imperfection factors for lateral torsional buckling curves

Buckling Curve	**a**	**b**	**c**	**d**
Imperfection factor α_{LT}	0.21	0.34	0.49	0.76

6.3.2.3(1)

NA.2.17

3. Recommendations for the buckling curves are given in Table 6.6.

Table 6.6 Recommendations for the selection of lateral torsional buckling curve

Cross-section	Limits	Buckling Curve
Rolled doubly symmetric I and H sections, and hot finished hollow sections	$h/b \leq 2$	b
	$2 < h/b \leq 3.1$	c
	$h/b > 3.1$	d
Angles (for moments in the major principal plane)		d
All other hot-rolled sections		d
Cold-formed hollow sections	$h/b \leq 2$	c
	$h/b > 2$	d

6.3.2.3(2)

Values of the reduction factor χ_{LT} for the appropriate non-dimensional slenderness $\bar{\lambda}_{LT}$ may be obtained from Figure 6.2.

Values of χ_{LT} may alternatively be determined from Table 6.7 below.

The reduction factor may be modified (increasing its value) to take into account the effect of the moment distribution between lateral restraints.

Note: Figure 6.2 and Table 6.7 are based on the expression for χ_{LT} given in 6.3.2.3(1)

Figure 6.2 Lateral torsional buckling curves for rolled sections

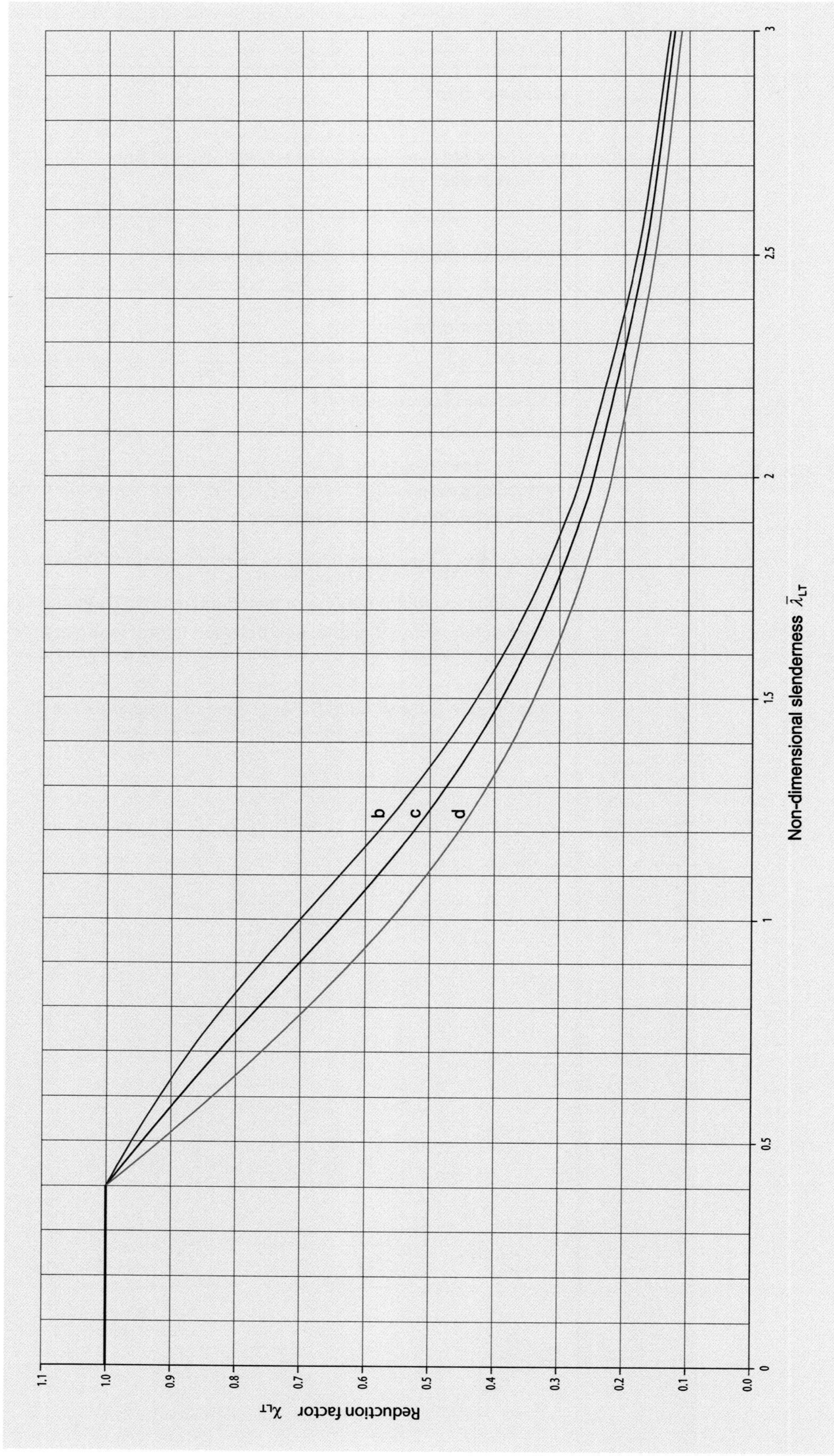

Table 6.7 Lateral torsional buckling reduction factors χ_{LT}

$\bar{\lambda}_{LT}$	Rolled I, H Sections		
	$h/b \leq 2$	$2 < h/b \leq 3.1$	$h/b > 3.1$
0.20	1.00	1.00	1.00
0.25	1.00	1.00	1.00
0.30	1.00	1.00	1.00
0.35	1.00	1.00	1.00
0.40	1.00	1.00	1.00
0.45	0.98	0.97	0.96
0.50	0.96	0.94	0.92
0.55	0.94	0.92	0.88
0.60	0.92	0.89	0.84
0.65	0.89	0.86	0.80
0.70	0.87	0.83	0.76
0.75	0.84	0.79	0.72
0.80	0.82	0.76	0.69
0.85	0.79	0.73	0.65
0.90	0.76	0.70	0.62
0.95	0.73	0.67	0.59
1.00	0.70	0.64	0.56
1.05	0.67	0.61	0.53
1.10	0.64	0.58	0.50
1.15	0.61	0.55	0.48
1.20	0.58	0.52	0.46
1.25	0.55	0.50	0.43
1.30	0.52	0.47	0.41
1.35	0.50	0.45	0.39
1.40	0.47	0.43	0.37
1.45	0.45	0.41	0.36
1.50	0.43	0.39	0.34
1.60	0.39	0.35	0.31
1.70	0.35	0.32	0.28
1.80	0.32	0.29	0.26
1.90	0.29	0.27	0.24
2.00	0.27	0.25	0.22
2.50	0.18	0.17	0.15
3.00	0.13	0.12	0.11

6.3.3 Uniform members in bending and axial compression

6.3.3(3)

1. For members of structural systems, verification of buckling resistance of doubly symmetric cross-sections may be carried out on the basis of the individual single span members regarded as cut out of the system. Second order effects of the sway system (P-Δ effects) should be taken into account, either by the end moments of the member or by means of appropriate buckling lengths about each axis for the global buckling mode.

6.3.3(4)

2. Members which are subjected to combined bending and axial compression should satisfy:

Developed from (6.61)

$$\frac{N_{Ed}}{N_{b,y,Rd}} + k_{yy}\frac{M_{y,Ed}}{M_{b,Rd}} + k_{yz}\frac{M_{z,Ed}}{M_{c,z,Rd}} \leq 1$$

Developed from (6.62)

$$\frac{N_{Ed}}{N_{b,z,Rd}} + k_{zy}\frac{M_{y,Ed}}{M_{b,Rd}} + k_{zz}\frac{M_{z,Ed}}{M_{c,z,Rd}} \leq 1$$

where:

N_{Ed}, $M_{y,Ed}$ and $M_{z,Ed}$	are the design values of the compression force and the maximum moments about the y-y and z-z axes along the member, respectively
$N_{b,y,Rd}$ and $N_{b,z,Rd}$	are the design buckling resistances of the member about the major and minor axis respectively from 6.3.1.1 (2)
$M_{b,Rd}$	is the design buckling resistance moment from 6.3.2.1(3)
$M_{c,z,Rd}$	$= \frac{W_{pl,z} f_y}{\gamma_{M1}}$ for Class 1 and 2 sections
	$= \frac{W_{el,z} f_y}{\gamma_{M1}}$ for Class 3 sections
k_{yy}, k_{yz}, k_{zy}, k_{zz}	are interaction factors, which may be determined from Annex A or B of BS EN 1993-1-1. Values are given in Annex D of this publication.

Note: ***The above criteria are based on the expressions in Clause 6.3.3(4) of BS EN 1993-1-1, interpreted in accordance with ECCS TC8 Rules for Member Stability in EN 1993-1-1 Background documentation and design guidelines.***

Annex B is recommended as the simpler approach for manual calculations. Use of either Annex is permitted by the National Annex.

In some cases, a conservative value of the k factors may be sufficient for initial design. The following table gives maximum values, based on Annex B of the Standard, and assuming the sections are susceptible to torsional deformations (i.e. not hollow sections).

Interaction Factor	Maximum Values	
	Class 3	Class 1 and 2
k_{yy}	$C_{my} \times 1.6$	$C_{my} \times 1.8$
k_{yz}	k_{zz}	$0.6 \times k_{zz}$
k_{zy}	1.0	1.0
k_{zz}	$C_{mz} \times 1.6$	$C_{mz} \times 2.4$

The equations to calculate the interaction factors are given in Appendix D of this publication. Appendix D also includes a series of graphs from which accurate values of the interaction factors may be determined as an alternative to calculation. Use of the graphs requires the non-dimensional slenderness, $\bar{\lambda}$ and the ratio of applied load / resistance, i.e. $\left(\frac{N_{Ed}}{N_{Rd}}\right)$.

6.3.4 Columns in simple construction

The rules in this clause are based on the NCCI document SN048 (available from www.steel-ncci.com), noting that the symbols used below are slightly different.

1. When the criteria given in 6.3.4(2) are satisfied a column in simple construction subject to combined bending and axial compression may be verified against buckling failure as follows:

$$\frac{N_{Ed}}{N_{min,b,Rd}} + \frac{M_{y,Ed}}{M_{b,Rd}} + 1.5\frac{M_{z,Ed}}{M_{cb,z,Rd}} \leq 1$$

where:

N_{Ed}, $M_{y,Ed}$ and $M_{z,Ed}$ are the design values of the compression force and the maximum design bending moments about the y-y and z-z axes along the member.

$N_{min,b,Rd}$ is the lesser of $\frac{\chi_y A f_y}{\gamma_{M1}}$ and $\frac{\chi_z A f_y}{\gamma_{M1}}$

$$M_{b,Rd} = \chi_{LT}\frac{W_{pl,y} f_y}{\gamma_{M1}}$$

$$M_{cb,z,Rd} = \frac{W_{pl,z} f_y}{\gamma_{M1}}$$

2. The following criteria must be satisfied to use the verification given in (1):

- The column is a hot rolled I or H section
- The cross-section is Class 1, 2 or 3 under compression
- The bending moment diagram about each axis is linear
- The column is restrained laterally in both the y-y and z-z directions at each floor but is unrestrained between floors
- $\psi \leq -0.11$ (where ψ is the ratio of the moments at the two ends).
- For a pin ended column ($\psi = 0$) the following alternative criterion must be satisfied to use the simplified interaction expression:

$$\frac{N_{\mathrm{Ed}}}{N_{\mathrm{b,y,Rd}}} \leq 0.83 \text{ in which } N_{\mathrm{b,y,Rd}} = \frac{\chi_{\mathrm{y}} A f_{\mathrm{y}}}{\gamma_{\mathrm{M1}}}$$ (the resistance in the major axis)

Note: $\psi = 0$ if there is a true pin at one end of the column (such as a base). In this case the simplified interaction expression is only valid if the axial force in the column is less than 83% of its resistance in the major axis.

3. Where the criteria in 6.3.4(2) are not satisfied the method given in 6.3.3 should be used.

4. The design bending moments should be determined by considering the vertical beam reactions to act at a distance of 100 mm from the face of the column (web or flange).

Note: The guidance given above has been derived from Annex B of BS EN 1993-1-1:2005.

6.4 Composite beams

This Section presents information that may be used in the design of composite beams; it does not contain detailed design guidance or rules because composite beams will normally be designed using software. For detailed design guidance refer to SCI publications, P300 and P359. A composite beam checking tool created by SCI is available from www.steelconstruction.info.

6.4.1 Initial beam sizing

Document SN022a-EN-GB (available from www.steelbiz.org) presents span to depth graphs that may be used to determine an initial beam size.

6.4.2 Material properties

Care should be taken when using the *design value of the cylinder compressive strength of concrete* (f_{cd}) as the definition in BS EN 1992-1-1 is not the same as that given in BS EN 1994-1-1.

BS EN 1992-1-1
3.1.6(1)

BS EN 1992-1-1 $$f_{cd} = \alpha_{cc} \frac{f_{ck}}{\gamma_C}$$

BS EN 1994-1-1
2.4.1.2(2)

BS EN 1994-1-1 $$f_{cd} = \frac{f_{ck}}{\gamma_C}$$

The definition of f_{cd} used should be that taken from the same Eurocode as the equation it is used in. In the UK, BS EN 1992-1-1 and BS EN 1994-1-1 give the same value for the plastic resistance. The NA to BS EN 1992-1-1 gives the values $\gamma_c = 1.5$ and $\alpha_{cc} = 0.85$

6.4.3 Verifications at SLS

BS EN 1994-1-1
5.4.2.2(11)

1. For buildings not intended mainly for storage, the effects of creep in concrete may be taken in to account by using an effective modulus of elasticity for concrete, $E_{c,eff} = E_{cm} / 2$.

6.4.4 Natural frequency

Guidance on determining the natural frequency of a composite beam is given in *Design of floors for vibration: A new approach* (SCI publication P354).

6.5 Web resistance to transverse forces

References given in the margin for this Section are to BS EN 1993-1-5: Plated structural elements. These are the only rules from that part of BS EN 1993 included in this guide.

6.5.1 Basis

6.1(1)

1. The design resistance of the webs of rolled beams should be determined in accordance with 6.5.2, provided that the compression flange is adequately restrained in the lateral direction.

6.1(2)

2. The load is applied as follows:
   - Through the flange and resisted by shear forces in the web, see Figure 6.3(a)
   - Through one flange and transferred through the web directly to the other flange, see Figure 6.3(b), or
   - Through one flange adjacent to an unstiffened end, see Figure 6.3(c).

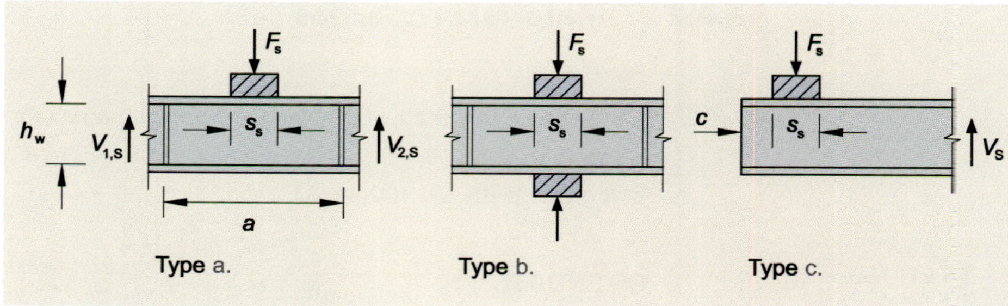

Figure 6.3 Load application types

Based on 6.6(1)

3. For a web resisting transverse forces, verify that:

$$\frac{F_{Ed}}{F_{Rd}} \leq 1.0$$

where:

F_{Ed} is the design transverse force applied to the web

F_{Rd} is the design resistance of the web to local buckling under transverse forces (see 6.5.2)

6.5.2 Design resistance

6.2(1)

1. For unstiffened or stiffened webs the design resistance to local buckling under transverse forces should be taken as:

$$F_{Rd} = \frac{f_{yw} L_{eff} t_w}{\gamma_{M1}}$$

where:

f_{yw} is the yield strength of the web

t_w is the thickness of the web

L_{eff} is the effective length for resistance to transverse forces

L_{eff} $= \chi_F \ell_y$

where:

χ_F is the reduction factor due to local buckling, see 6.5.4

ℓ_y is the effective loaded length, appropriate to the length of stiff bearing, see 6.5.5.

6.5.3 Length of stiff bearing

6.3(1), 6.3(3)

1. The length of stiff bearing s_s on the flange should be taken as the distance over which the applied load is effectively distributed at a slope of 1:1, see Figure 6.4. However, s_s should not be taken as larger than h_w and where the applied load rests at an angle to the flange surface, ss should be taken as zero.

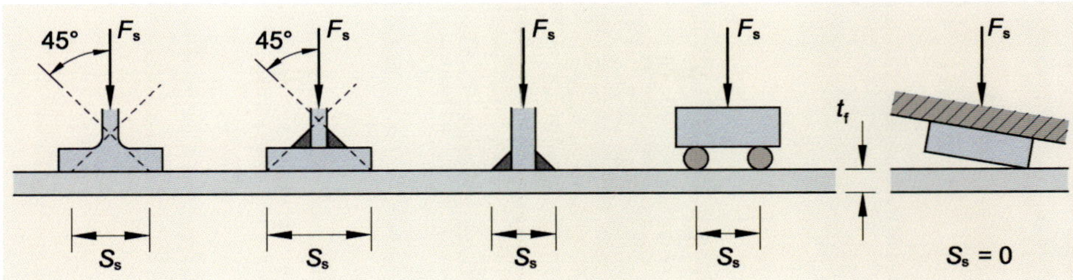

Figure 6.4 Length of stiff bearing

↖ 6.3(2)

2. If several concentrated forces are closely spaced, the resistance should be checked for each individual force as well as for the total load with s_s as the centre-to-centre distance between the outer loads.

6.5.4 Reduction factor for effective length for resistance

↖ 6.4(1)

1. The reduction factor χ_F should be obtained from:

$$\chi_F = \frac{0.5}{\bar{\lambda}_F} \le 1.0$$

where:

$$\bar{\lambda}_F = \sqrt{\frac{\ell_y t_w f_{yw}}{F_{cr}}}$$

$$F_{cr} = 0.9\, k_F E \frac{t_w^{\,3}}{h_w}$$

↖ 6.4(2) and formulae extracted from Figure 6.1

2. For webs without longitudinal stiffeners k_F should be determined from:

Type (a) $\quad k_F = 6 + 2\left(\frac{h_w}{a}\right)^2$

Type (b) $\quad k_F = 3.5 + 2\left(\frac{h_w}{a}\right)^2$

Type (c) $\quad k_F = 2 + 6\left(\frac{s_s + c}{h_w}\right) \le 6$

6.5.5 Effective loaded length

↖ Reordered paragraphs from 6.5

1. The effective loaded length (ℓ_y) should be calculated as follows:
   a. For load application types (a) and (b) in Figure 6.3 ℓ_y should be obtained using:

   $$\ell_y = s_s + 2t_f\left(1 + \sqrt{m_1 + m_2}\right)$$

   but $\ell_y \le$ distance between adjacent transverse stiffeners
   b. For load application type (c) in Figure 6.3 ℓ_y should be taken as the smallest value obtained from the expression given in a) and the following expressions:

$$\ell_y = \ell_e + t_f \sqrt{\frac{m_1}{2} + \left(\frac{\ell_e}{t_f}\right)^2 + m_2}$$

$$\ell_y = \ell_e + t_f \sqrt{m_1 + m_2}$$

where:

$$\ell_e = \frac{k_F E t_w^{\ 2}}{2 f_{yw} h_w} \leq s_s + c$$

6.5(1)

2. m_1 and m_2 should be calculated as:

$m_1 = \dfrac{f_{yf} b_f}{f_{yw} t_w}$ in which b_f is the width of the flange

$m_2 = 0.02\left(\dfrac{h_w}{t_f}\right)^2$ if $\overline{\lambda}_F > 0.5$

$m_2 = 0.0$ if $\overline{\lambda}_F \leq 0.5$

6.5.6 Bearing stiffeners

9.4(1)

1. If the design resistance of an unstiffened web is insufficient for transverse loads, transverse stiffeners should be provided.

9.1(3)

2. When checking the buckling resistance, the section of a stiffener may be taken as the gross area of the stiffener plus a width of plate equal to $15\varepsilon t$ (= $13.8t$ for S275, $12.1t$ for S355 and $10.7t$ for S460) but not more than the actual dimension available, on each side of the stiffener. See Figure 6.5.

Note: ***The above rule in BS EN 1993-1-5, 9.1(3) applies to single stiffeners on one face (for the restraint of the web against shear buckling) and to stiffeners on both faces (for carrying transverse loads). In this guide, the only stiffeners covered are those with a single flat on each face, as shown in Figure 6.5.***

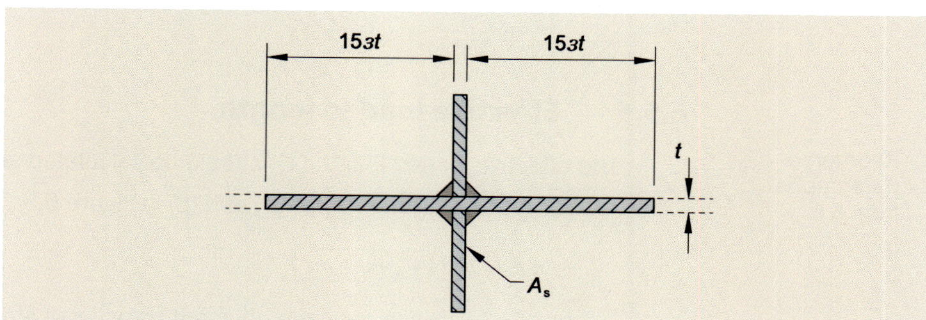

Figure 6.5 Effective area of stiffener

9.4(2)

3. The out-of-plane buckling resistance of the transverse stiffener under transverse loads should be determined from 6.3.3 using buckling curve c. When both ends are assumed to be fixed laterally a buckling length l of not less than $0.75\ h_w$ should be used. A larger value of l should be used for conditions that provide less end restraint. If the stiffeners have cut outs at the loaded end, the cross-sectional resistance should be checked at this end.

6.6 Triangulated structures

References given in the margin for this Section are to BS EN 1993-1-1 and its National Annex unless otherwise noted.

6.6.1 General

BS EN 1993-1-8 5.1.5(2)

1. The distribution of axial forces in a lattice girder may be determined on the assumption that the members are connected by pinned joints.

BB.1.1(1)B

2. For chord members generally and for out-of-plane buckling of web members, the buckling length L_{cr} may be taken as equal to the system length L, unless a smaller value can be justified by analysis.

> The in-plane system lengths of chord members (rafters or bottom chords) should be taken as the distance between connections to internal members, and the out-of-plane lengths as the distance between purlins or longitudinal ties, provided that such ties are properly connected to an adequate restraint system.

BB.1.1(2)B

3. The buckling length L_{cr} of an I or H section chord member may be taken as $0.9L$ for in-plane buckling and $1.0L$ for out-of-plane buckling, unless a smaller value is justified by analysis.

BB.1.1(3)

4. Web members may be designed for in-plane buckling using a buckling length smaller than the system length, provided the chords supply appropriate end restraint and the end connections supply appropriate fixity (at least two bolts if bolted).

BB.1.1(4)

5. Under these conditions, in normal triangulated structures the buckling length L_{cr} of web members for in-plane buckling may be taken as $0.9L$, except for angle sections, see 6.6.2.

6.6.2 Angles as web members

6.6.2.1 *In-plane slenderness ratios for angle web members*

BB.1.2(1)B

1. Provided that the chords provide appropriate end restraint to web members made of angles and the end connections of such web members supply appropriate fixity (at least two bolts if bolted), the eccentricities may be neglected and end fixities allowed for in the design of angles as web members in compression. The effective slenderness ratio $\bar{\lambda}_{eff}$ may be obtained as follows:

$$\bar{\lambda}_{eff,v} = 0.35 + 0.7\bar{\lambda}_{v}$$ for buckling about v-v axis

(BB.1)

$$\bar{\lambda}_{eff,y} = 0.50 + 0.7\bar{\lambda}_{y}$$ for buckling about y-y axis

$$\bar{\lambda}_{eff,z} = 0.50 + 0.7\bar{\lambda}_{z}$$ for buckling about z-z axis

where:

$\bar{\lambda}$ is as defined in 6.3.1.2

BB.1.2(2)B

2. When only one bolt is used for end connections of angle web members the eccentricity should be taken into account using 6.2.8 and the buckling length L_{cr} should be taken as equal to the system length L.

SERVICEABILITY LIMIT STATES

References given in the margin for this Section are to BS EN 1990 and its National Annex unless noted otherwise.

7.1 Basis

A1.4.2(2) and BS EN 1993-1-1, 7.2

1. The serviceability criteria should be specified for each project and agreed with the client.

Suggested vertical and horizontal deflection limits are given in Table 7.1 and Table 7.2. Guidance on limits for dynamic performance are given in *Design of floors for vibration: A new approach* (SCI publication P354).

A1.4.3(6)

2. Long term deformations due to shrinkage, relaxation or creep should be considered where relevant, and calculated by using the effects of the permanent actions and quasi permanent values of the variable actions ($\psi_{2,i} Q_{k,i}$).

7.2 Vertical deflections

A1.4.3(3)

1. If the functioning or damage of the structure or to finishes, or to non-structural members (e.g. partition walls, claddings) is being considered, the verification for deflection should take account of those effects of permanent and variable actions that occur after the execution of the member or finish concerned.

However, in some circumstances it may be appropriate to consider the permanent actions that occur during the execution of the structure, i.e. an exposed beam that only supports cladding or brickwork.

BS EN 1993-1-1 NA.2.23

2. On low pitch and flat roofs the possibility of ponding due to vertical deflection should be investigated.

7.2.1 Steel members

BS EN 1993-1-1 NA.2.23

1. Table 7.1 gives suggested limits for calculated vertical deflections of certain members under the characteristic load combination due to variable loads alone. Circumstances may arise where greater or lesser values would be more appropriate. Other members may also need deflection limits.

BS EN 1993-1-1
NA.2.2.3

Table 7.1 Suggested limits for vertical deflection due to characteristic combination (variable actions only)

Vertical Deflection	
Cantilever	Length/180
Beams carrying plaster or other brittle finish	Span/360
Other beams (except purlins and sheeting rails)	Span/200
Purlins and sheeting rails	To suit the characteristics of the particular cladding

7.2.2 Steel and concrete composite beams

The limits for vertical deflection of composite beams under the variable actions only should be taken from Table 7.1. When the structure is not mainly intended for storage, and the effects of deformed geometry are not significant ($\alpha_{cr} \geq 10$), the deflections under all loads can be calculated using an effective modulus of elasticity for concrete of $E_{c,eff} = E_{cm}/2$, where E_{cm} is the short-term secant modulus of elasticity (BS EN 1994-1-1, 5.4.2.2(11)).

7.2.3 Steel and concrete composite floors

The deflection limits that should be used for composite floors during execution are:

When ponding is not explicitly considered: $\dfrac{\text{effective span}}{180}$ but ≤ 20 mm

When ponding is explicitly considered: $\dfrac{\text{effective span}}{130}$ but ≤ 30 mm

At the normal stage, the deflection can be calculated using the average of the cracked and uncracked second moment of areas (BS EN 1994-1-1, 9.8.2(5)), and should be limited to effective span/500 for the quasi-permanent actions (BS EN 1992-1-1, 7.4.1(5)).

7.3 Horizontal deflections

BS EN 1993-1-1 NA.2.2.4

1. Table 7.2 gives suggested limits for calculated horizontal deflections of certain members under the characteristic load combination due to variable load. Circumstances may arise where greater or lesser values would be more appropriate. Other members may also need deflection limits.

Table 7.2 Suggested limits for horizontal deflection

Horizontal Deflection	
Tops of columns in single-storey buildings except portal frames	Height/300
Columns in portal frame buildings, not supporting crane runways	To suit the characteristics of the particular cladding
In each storey of a building with more than one storey	Height of that storey/300

7.4 Dynamics

A1.4.4(1)

1. To achieve satisfactory dynamic behaviour of buildings and their structural members under serviceability conditions, the following aspects, amongst others, should be considered:
   - the comfort of the user
   - the functioning of the structure or its structural members (e.g. cracks in partitions, damage to cladding, sensitivity of building contents to vibrations).

   Other aspects should be considered for each project and agreed with the client.

A1.4.4(2)

2. For the serviceability limit state of a structure or a structural member not to be exceeded when subjected to vibrations, a very simplistic but widely adopted approach is to ensure that the natural frequency of vibrations of the structure or structural member is kept above appropriate values which depend upon the function of the building and the source of the vibration, and are agreed with the client and/or the relevant authority.

A1.4.4(3)

3. It will often be beneficial to carry out a more refined analysis of the dynamic response of the structure, including consideration of damping.

   Note: For further guidance, see EN 1991-1-1, EN 1991-1-4 and ISO 10137.

A1.4.4(4)

4. Possible sources of vibration that should be considered include walking, synchronised movements of people, machinery, ground borne vibrations from traffic, and wind actions. These, and other sources, should be specified for each project and agreed with the client.

Note: Guidance on the design of floors for vibration is given in SCI publication P354.

CONNECTIONS

In this Section, marginal references are to BS EN 1993-1-8 and its National Annex unless noted otherwise.

For basis of design for joints, see Section 2.5.

BS EN 1993-1-8 describes joints and connections. A joint is the zone where two or more members meet, and includes, in a beam to column joint for example, the column web panel. A *connection* is defined as the location where two or more elements meet. In the example of the beam to column joint, the connection refers to the collection of components such as the end plate, column flange, welds and bolts. The joint comprises the connection plus the column web panel.

8.1 Analysis, classification and modelling

8.1.1 Global analysis

5.1.1(1) 1. The effects of the behaviour of the joints on the distribution of internal forces and moments within a structure, and on the overall deformations of the structure, should generally be taken into account, but where these effects are sufficiently small they may be neglected.

5.1.1(2) 2. To identify whether the effects of joint behaviour on the analysis need to be taken into account, a distinction may be made between three simplified joint models as follows:

- simple, in which the joint may be assumed not to transmit bending moments
- continuous, in which the behaviour of the joint may be assumed to have no effect on the analysis
- semi-continuous, in which the behaviour of the joint needs to be taken into account in the analysis.

5.1.1(3) 3. The appropriate type of joint model should be determined from Table 8.1.

Table 8.1 Type of joint model

Method of Global Analysis	Classification of Joint	Type of Joint Model
Elastic	Nominally pinned	Simple
	Rigid	Continuous
	Semi-rigid	Semi-continuous

> Note: *The Table 8.1 is a re-presentation of part of Table 5.1 in BS EN 1993-1-8. It is limited to classifications appropriate to elastic global analysis, as this is the common case for general frame analysis. Plastic analysis is outside the scope of this guide.*

8.1.2 Global analysis of lattice girders

5.1.5(2)

1. The distribution of axial forces in a lattice girder may be determined on the assumption that the members are connected by pinned joints.

5.1.5(3)

2. Secondary moments at the joints, caused by the rotational stiffness of the joints, may be neglected both in the design of the members and in the design of the joints provided that certain conditions are satisfied.

> The conditions when secondary moments can be neglected require that hollow section joints fall within the scope of BS EN 1993-1-8 (Section 7). The second important qualification is that the ratio of the system length to the depth of the member in the plane of the lattice girder is not less than the appropriate minimum values – which for buildings may be assumed to be 6.

5.1.5(4)

3. The moments resulting from transverse loads that are applied between panel points, should be taken into account in the design of the members to which they are applied.
   - the brace members may be considered as pin-connected to the chords, so moments resulting from transverse loads applied to chord members need not be distributed into brace members.
   - the chords may be considered as continuous beams, with simple supports at panel points.

> In Clause 5.1.5(6) BS EN 1993-1-8 provides limits when the effects of nodal eccentricities may be neglected in hollow section lattice girders.

8.1.3 Classification of joints

5.2.1

1. The details of all joints should fulfil the assumptions made in the relevant design method, without adversely affecting any other part of the structure.
2. Joints may be classified by their stiffness and by their strength.

> For elastic global analysis, joints should be classified on the basis of their stiffness. The Standard offers a calculation approach in Clause 6.1.2. The Standard also notes that alternative approaches to classification are permitted, in Clause 5.2.2.1(2).

5.2.2.1(2)

3. A joint may be classified on the basis of experimental evidence, experience of previous satisfactory performance in similar cases or by calculations based on test evidence.

NA 2.6

> The National Annex to BS EN 1991-1-8 states that connections designed in accordance with the principles given in *Joints in steel construction – Simple joints to Eurocode 3* (SCI publication P358) may be classified as nominally pinned joints. Connections designed in accordance with the principles given in *Joints in steel construction – Moment resisting joints to Eurocode 3* (SCI publication P398) may be classified on the basis of the guidance given in Section 2.5 of the same publication.
>
> This guidance obviates the need for the calculation of stiffness – as long as the connections follow the principles in the referenced publications.

8.2 Bolted connections

8.2.1 General

3.1.1(1)

1. All bolts, nuts and washers should comply with the standards listed in 4.2.1
2. The yield strength f_{yb} and the ultimate tensile strength f_{ub} for bolt Classes 4.6 and 8.8 are given in Section 4.2.1(3).

8.2.2 Preloaded bolts

3.1.2(1)

1. Only bolt assemblies of Class 8.8 and Class 10.9 conforming to the requirements given in the standards for preloaded bolts in 4.2.1, with controlled tightening in accordance with the requirements in BS EN 1090-2, may be used as preloaded bolts.

> In the UK, only system HR and system HRC bolts are used as preloaded bolts. System HV bolts (to BS EN 14399-4) are **not** used in the UK.

8.2.3 Categories of bolted connections

3.4.1(1)

1. Bolted connections loaded in shear should be designed as one of the following:
   - Category A: Bearing type
   - Category B: Slip-resistant at serviceability limit state
   - Category C: Slip-resistant at ultimate limit state

   Note that for Category C connections where the connected elements are in tension, the design plastic resistance of the net cross section at bolt holes (see 6.2.3) should also be verified.

   The design checks for these connections are summarised in Table 8.2.

3.4.2(1)

2. Bolted connections loaded in tension should be designed as one of the following:
   - Category D: Non-preloaded
   - Category E: Preloaded

   The design checks for these connections are summarised in Table 8.2.

Table 3.2

Table 8.2 Categories of bolted connections

Category	Criteria	Remarks
Shear Connections		
A Bearing type	$F_{v,Ed} \leq F_{v,Rd}$ $F_{v,Ed} \leq F_{b,Rd}$	No preloading required. Bolt classes 4.6, 8.8 & 10.9
B Slip-resistant at serviceability limit state	$F_{v,Ed,ser} \leq F_{s,Rd,ser}$ $F_{v,Ed} \leq F_{v,Rd}$ $F_{v,Ed} \leq F_{b,Rd}$	Preloaded 8.8 or 10.9 bolts should be used. For slip resistance at serviceability see 8.2.8.1
C Slip-resistant at ultimate limit state	$F_{v,Ed} \leq F_{s,Rd}$ $F_{v,Ed} \leq F_{b,Rd}$ $F_{v,Ed} \leq N_{net,Rd}$	Preloaded 8.8 or 10.9 bolts should be used. For slip resistance at serviceability see 8.2.8.1 See note to 8.2.3(1)
Tension Connections		
D Non-preloaded	$F_{t,Ed} \leq F_{t,Rd}$ $F_{t,Ed} \leq B_{p,Rd}$	No preloading required. Bolt classes 4.6, 8.8 & 10.9
E Preloaded	$F_{t,Ed} \leq F_{t,Rd}$ $F_{t,Ed} \leq B_{p,Rd}$	Preloaded 8.8 or 10.9 bolts should be used.

The design tensile force $F_{t,Ed}$ should include any force due to prying action, see 8.2.10. Bolts subject to both shear force and tensile force should also satisfy the criteria given in Table 8.4. However, AD 354 provides a simple method of determining the design tension resistance of bolted connections that avoids the need to evaluate prying forces, based on the simple method provided in BS 5950-1:2000.

2.6(3)

3. For wind and stability bracings, bolts in Category A connections may be used.

3.4.2(1)(a)

4. Category D connections may be used in connections designed to resist normal wind loads.

> Non preloaded bolts may be used in bracing connections.

8.2.4 Positioning holes for bolts

3.5(1)

1. Minimum and maximum spacing and end and edge distances for bolts are given in Table 8.3.

Table 3.3

Table 8.3 Minimum and maximum spacing, end and edge distances

Distances and spacings, see Figure 8.1	Minimum	Maximum [1] [2] [3]	
		Steel exposed to weather or other corrosive influences	Steel not exposed to weather or other corrosive influences
Edge distance e_1	$1.2\ d_0$	$4t + 40$ mm	
Edge distance e_2	$1.2\ d_0$	$4t + 40$ mm	
Spacing p_1	$2.2\ d_0$	The smaller of $14t$ or 200 mm	The smaller of $14t$ or 200 mm
Spacing p_2	$2.4\ d_0$	The smaller of $14t$ or 200 mm	The smaller of $14t$ or 200 mm

[1] Maximum values for spacings, edge and end distances are unlimited, except in the following cases:
- for compression members in order to avoid local buckling and to prevent corrosion in exposed members and;
- for exposed tension members to prevent corrosion.

[2] The local buckling resistance of the plate in compression between fasteners should be calculated according to 6.3 using $0.6p_1$ as buckling length. Local buckling between the fasteners need not be checked if p_1/t is smaller than 9ε. The edge distance should not exceed the local buckling requirements for an outstand element in the compression members, see Table 5.1. The end distance is not affected by this requirement.

[3] t is the thickness of the thinner outer connected part.

[4] d_0 is the diameter of the hole

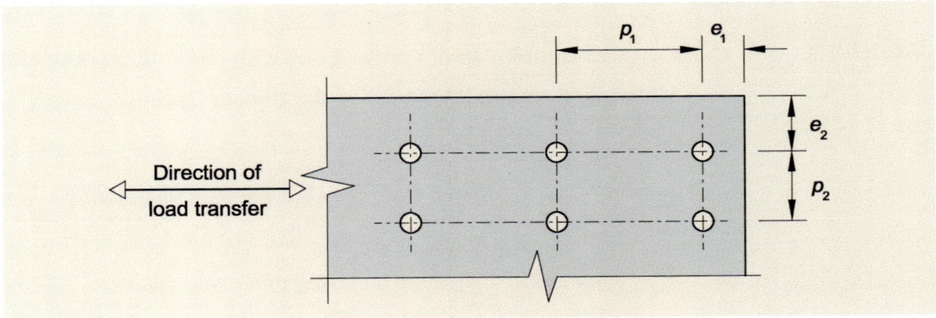

Figure 8.1 Symbols for spacing of fasteners

BS EN 1993-1-8 provides information on the spacing of staggered holes in Clause 3.5.

8.2.5 Design resistance of individual bolts

3.6.1(1)

1. The design resistance for an individual bolt subjected to shear and/or tension is given in Table 8.4.

3.6.1(3)

2. The design resistances for tension and for shear through the threaded portion of a bolt given in Table 8.4 should only be used for bolts manufactured in conformity with the standards listed in 4.2.1.

3.6.1(4)

3. The design shear resistance $F_{v,Rd}$ given in Table 8.4 should only be used where the bolts are used in holes with nominal clearances not exceeding those for normal holes as specified in BS EN 1090-2.

> For M16, M20 and M24 bolts, the nominal hole diameter is 2 mm larger than the bolt diameter.

3.6.1(10)

4. In single lap joints with only one bolt row (see Figure 8.2), the bolts should be provided with washers under both the head and the nut. The design bearing resistance $F_{b,Rd}$ for each bolt should be limited to:

   $F_{b,Rd} \leq 1.5 f_u \, dt/\gamma_{M2}$

3.6.1(11)

5. In the case of Class 8.8 bolts, hardened washers should be used for single lap joints with only one bolt or one row of bolts.

3.6.1(12)

6. Where bolts transmitting load in shear and bearing pass through packing of total thickness t_p greater than one-third of the nominal diameter d (see Figure 8.3), the design shear resistance $F_{v,Rd}$ calculated as specified in Table 8.4, should be multiplied by a reduction factor β_p given by:

   $$\beta_p = \frac{9d}{8d + 3t_p} \quad \text{but } \beta_p \leq 1$$

> Although no upper limit to packing thickness is given in BS EN 1993-1-8, it is recommended that the thickness should not exceed $4d/3$, as stated in BS 5950-1.

3.6.1(13)

7. For double shear connections with packing on both sides of the splice, t_p should be taken as the thickness of the thicker packing.

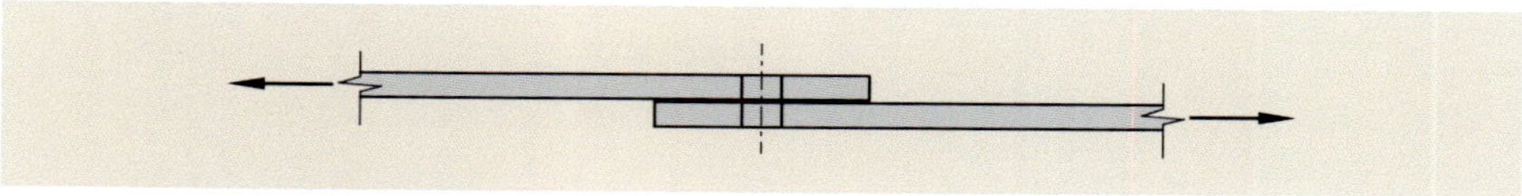

Figure 8.2 Single lap joint with one row of bolts

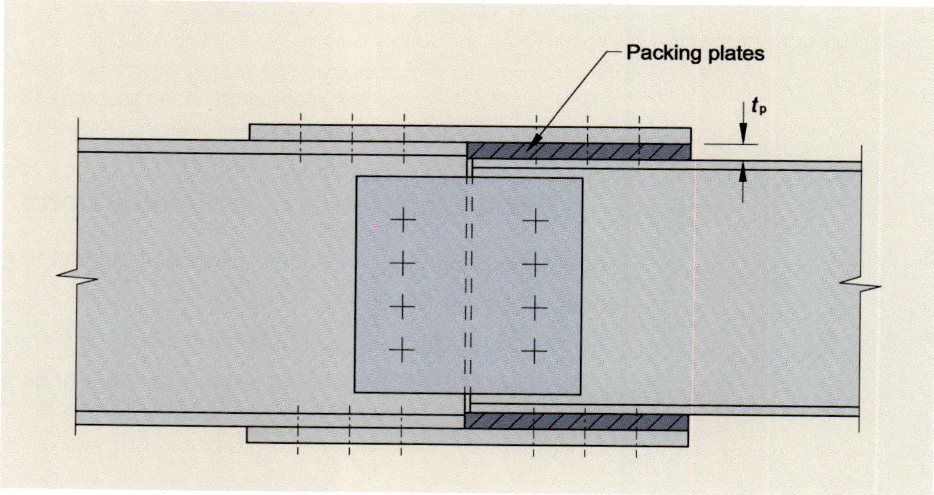

Figure 8.3 Fasteners through packings

Table 3.4

Table 8.4 Design resistance for individual fasteners subject to shear and/or tension

Failure Mode	Design Resistance
Shear resistance per shear plane	Where the shear plane passes through the threaded portion of the bolt: $F_{v,Rd} = \frac{0.6 f_{ub} A_s}{\gamma_{M2}}$ A_s is the tensile stress area of the bolt Where the shear plane passes through the unthreaded portion of the bolt: $F_{v,Rd} = \frac{0.6 f_{ub} A}{\gamma_{M2}}$ A is the gross cross-sectional area of the bolt.
Bearing resistance [1],[2],[3]	$F_{b,Rd} = \frac{k_1 \alpha_b f_u d t}{\gamma_{M2}}$ Where d is the nominal diameter of the bolt, α_b is the smallest of α_d, $\frac{f_{ub}}{f_u}$ or 1.0 For end bolts: $\alpha_d = \frac{e_1}{3d_0}$ For inner bolts $\alpha_d = \frac{p_1}{3d_0} - \frac{1}{4}$ For edge bolts k_1 is the smallest of $2.8\frac{e_2}{d_0} - 1.7$ or 2.5 For inner bolts k_1 is the smallest of $1.4\frac{p_2}{d_0} - 1.7$ or 2.5
Tension resistance [2]	$F_{t,Rd} = \frac{k_2 f_{ub} A_s}{\gamma_{M2}}$ where $k_2 = 0.63$ for countersunk bolts otherwise $k_2 = 0.9$
Punching shear resistance	$B_{p,Rd} = \frac{0.6 \pi d_m t_p f_u}{\gamma_{M2}}$
Combined shear and tension	$\frac{F_{v,Ed}}{F_{v,Rd}} + \frac{F_{t,Ed}}{1.4 F_{t,Rd}} \leq 1.0$

[1] The bearing resistance $F_{b,Rd}$ for bolts
- In oversized holes is 0.8 times the bearing resistance for bolts in normal holes.

[2] For a countersunk bolt:
- The bearing resistance $F_{b,Rd}$ should be based on a plate thickness t equal to the thickness of the connected plate minus half the depth of the countersinking.
- For the determination of the tension resistance, $F_{b,Rd}$ the angle and depth of countersinking should conform with the reference standards listed in 4.2.1. Otherwise the tension resistance $F_{t,Rd}$ should be adjusted accordingly.

[3] When the load on a bolt is not parallel to the edge, the bearing resistance may be verified separately for the bolt load components parallel and normal to the end.

The shear resistance of an M20 8.8 ordinary bolt (non-preloaded; Class A in Table 8.2) is 94.1 kN.

When the end distance, edge distance and pitch do not govern the bearing resistance, the bearing resistance is proportional to the material thickness. However, in many practical connections, the bearing resistance will be governed by the end or edge distance, or pitch, so the bearing resistance must be calculated.

8.2.6 Group of fasteners

3.7(1)

1. The design resistance of a group of fasteners may be taken as the sum of the design bearing resistances $F_{b,Rd}$ of the individual fasteners provided that the design shear resistance $F_{v,Rd}$ of each individual fastener is greater than or equal to the design bearing resistance $F_{b,Rd}$. Otherwise the design resistance of a group of fasteners should be taken as the number of fasteners multiplied by the smallest design resistance of any of the individual fasteners.

In any group of fasteners, the bearing resistances may vary (due to the end distance affecting the resistance of the end bolts). The shear resistance will be the same for each bolt. Consider three cases:

Case (i) The shear bearing resistances are less than the shear resistance - the resistance of the group is the sum of the individual bearing resistances.

Case (ii) The shear resistance is greater than some (but not all) bearing resistances in the group – the resistance of the connection is the minimum bearing resistance in the group, multiplied by the number of bolts.

Case (iii) The shear resistance is less than all the bearing resistances in the group – the resistance of the connection is the shear resistance of a bolt, multiplied by the number of bolts.

8.2.7 Long joints

3.8(1)

1. Where the distance L_j between the centres of the end fasteners in a joint, measured in the direction of force transfer (see Figure 8.4) is more than $15d$, the design shear resistance $F_{v,Rd}$ of all the fasteners calculated according to Table 8.4 should be multiplied by a reduction factor β_{Lf} given by:

$$\beta_{Lf} = 1 - \frac{L_j - 15d}{200d}$$

But $\beta_{Lf} \leq 1.0$ and $\beta_{Lf} \geq 0.75$

3.8(2)

2. The provision in 8.2.7(1) does not apply where there is a uniform distribution of force transfer over the length of the joint, e.g. the transfer of shear between the web and flange of a section.

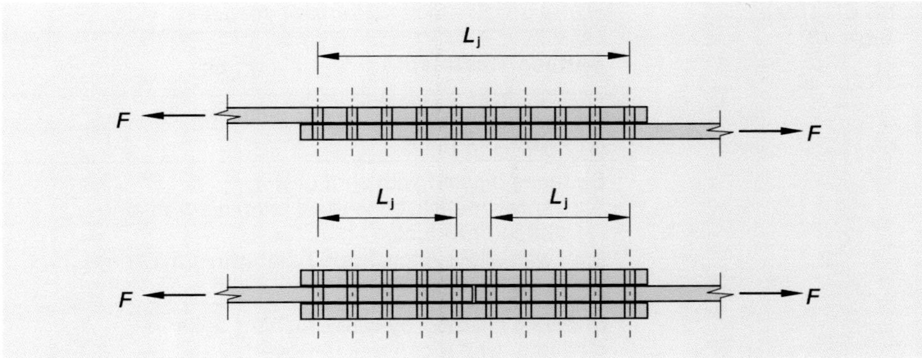

Figure 8.4 Long joints

8.2.8 Slip resistant connections

8.2.8.1 Design slip resistance

3.9.1(1)

1. The design slip resistance of a preloaded Class 8.8 bolt should be taken as:

$$F_{s,Rd} = \frac{k_s n \mu}{\lambda_{M3}} F_{p,C}$$

where:

k_s is given in Table 8.5

n is the number of the friction surfaces

μ is the slip factor as given in Table 8.6.

3.9.1(2)

2. For Class 8.8 bolts conforming with the reference standards for preloaded bolts in 4.2.1, with controlled tightening in conformity with EN 1090-2, the preloading force $F_{p,C}$ to be used in the expression in (1) should be taken as:

$$F_{p,C} = 0.7 f_{ub} A_s$$

Table 8.5 Values of k_s

Description	k_s
Bolts in normal holes	1.0
Bolts in either oversized holes or short slotted holes with the axis of the slot perpendicular to the direction of load transfer	0.85

BS EN 1090-2 Table 18

Table 8.6 Slip factor μ for preloaded bolts

Surface Treatment	Class of Friction Surfaces	Slip Factor μ
Surfaces blasted with shot or grit with loose rust removed, not pitted	A	0.5
Surfaces blasted with shot or grit: a. spray metallised with an aluminium or zinc based product; b. with alkali zinc silicate paint with a thickness of 50 μm to 80 μm	B	0.4
Surfaces cleaned by wire brushing or flame cleaning, with loose rust removed	C	0.3
Surfaces as rolled	D	0.2

Notes

[1] The requirements for testing and inspection are given in EN 1090-2.

[2] The classification of any other surface treatment should be based on test specimens representative of the surfaces used in the structure using the procedure set out in EN 1090-2.

[3] With painted surface treatments account should made for any loss of pre-load which occur over time.

8.2.9 Design for block tearing

3.10.2

1. Block tearing consists of failure in shear at the row of bolts along the shear face of the hole group accompanied by tensile rupture along the line of bolt holes on the tension face of the bolt group. Figure 8.5 shows block tearing.

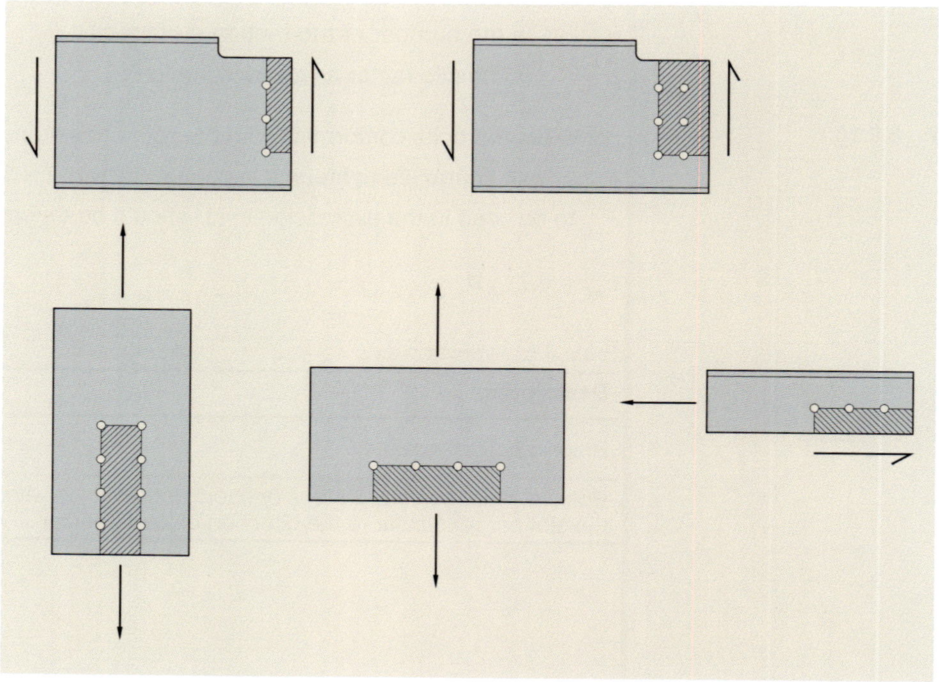

Figure 8.5 Examples of block tearing

3.10.2(1)

Note that in Figure 8.5, two examples show bolt groups subject to concentric loading; the remainder show bolt groups subject to eccentric loading.

3.10.2(2)

2. For a symmetric bolt group subject to concentric loading, the design block tearing resistance, $V_{eff,1,Rd}$ is given by:

(3.9)

$$V_{eff,1,Rd} = \frac{f_u A_{nt}}{\gamma_{M2}} + \frac{(1/\sqrt{3}) f_y A_{nv}}{\gamma_{M0}}$$

where:

A_{nt} is net area subject to tension;

A_{nv} is net area subject to shear.

3.10.2(3)

3. For a bolt group subject to eccentric loading, the design block shear tearing resistance $V_{eff,2,Rd}$ is given by:

(3.10)

$$V_{eff,2,Rd} = \frac{0.5 f_u A_{nt}}{\gamma_{M2}} + \frac{(1/\sqrt{3}) f_y A_{nv}}{\gamma_{M0}}$$

8.2.10 Prying

The design tension resistance ($F_{t,Rd}$) of individual fasteners is given by BS EN 1993-1-8 Table 3.4. In a tension connection, Clause 3.11 requires that the fasteners should be designed to resist a design tensile force ($F_{t,Ed}$) that includes any force due to prying action. Clause 6.2.4 provides rules (in Table 6.2) for T-stub flanges that implicitly account for prying forces.

In contrast, BS 5950-1 includes a simple method to verify the tension capacity of connections using bolts by utilising a reduced 'nominal tension capacity' (equal to 0.8 x the tension capacity) that is verified against a tensile force that excludes prying force. This means that, in certain circumstances, designers need not calculate the prying force. SCI (AD354) recommends that, for verifying resistance of a bolted tension connection when designing to BS EN 1993-1-8, as an alternative to the 'exact method' of Table 6.2, this simple approach may be adopted, provided that the cross-centres (gauge) of the bolt lines are not greater than 55% of the flange width or end plate width.

8.3 Welded connections

8.3.1 General

4.1(1)

1. The provisions in this section apply to weldable structural steels conforming to the standards in 4.1 and to material thickness of 4 mm and over.

4.1(1)

2. The provisions also apply to joints in which the mechanical properties of the weld metal are compatible with those of the parent metal.

8.3.2 Geometry and dimensions

8.3.2.1 Type of weld

1. This guide covers the design of fillet welds and butt welds.

8.3.2.2 Fillet welds

4.3.2.1(1) 1. Fillet welds may be used for connecting parts where the fusion faces form an angle of between 60° and 120°.

4.3.2.1(2) 2. Angles smaller than 60° are also permitted. However, in such cases the weld should be considered to be a partial penetration butt weld.

4.3.2.1(3) 3. For angles greater than 120° the resistance of fillet welds should be determined by testing in accordance with EN 1990 Annex D: Design by testing.

4.3.2.1(4) 4. Fillet welds finishing at the ends or sides of parts should be returned continuously, full size, around the corner for a distance of a least twice the leg length of the weld, unless access or the configuration of the joint renders this impractical. In the case of intermittent welds this rule applies only to the last intermittent fillet weld at corners.

4.3.2.1(5) 5. End returns should be indicated on the drawings.

4.3.2.1(6) 6. For eccentrically loaded single-sided fillet welds, see 8.3.8 of this guide.

8.3.2.3 Intermittent fillet welds

> Clause 4.3.2.2 of BS EN 1993-1-8 covers intermittent fillet welds, including setting out requirements and the provisions at the ends of runs. These should not be used in corrosive conditions and are generally inappropriate for the welded connections considered within the scope of this guide.

8.3.2.4 Butt welds

4.3.4(1) 1. A full penetration butt weld is defined as a weld that has complete penetration and fusion of weld and parent metal throughout the thickness of the joint.

4.3.4(2) 2. A partial penetration butt weld is defined as a weld that has joint penetration which is less than the full thickness of the parent material.

4.3.4(3) 3. Intermittent butt welds should not be used.

4.3.4(4) 4. For eccentricity in single-sided partial penetration butt welds, see 8.3.8 of this publication.

8.3.3 Design resistance of a fillet weld

8.3.3.1 Length of welds

4.5.1(1) 1. The effective length of a fillet weld l should be taken as the length over which the fillet is full size. This may be taken as the overall length of the weld reduced by twice the effective throat thickness a. Provided that the weld is full size throughout its length including starts and terminations, no reduction in effective length need be made for either the start or the termination of the weld.

4.5.1(2)

2. A fillet weld with an effective length less than 30 mm or less that six times the throat thickness, whichever is the larger, should not be designed to carry load.

8.3.3.2 Effective throat thickness

4.5.2(1)

1. The effective throat thickness, a, of a fillet weld should be taken as the height of the largest triangle (with equal or unequal legs) that can be inscribed within the fusion faces and the weld surface, measured perpendicular to the outer side of this triangle, see Figure 8.6.
2. The effective throat thickness of a fillet weld should not be less than 3 mm.

4.5.2(3)

3. In determining the design resistance of a deep penetration fillet weld, account may be taken of its additional throat thickness, see Figure 8.7, provided that preliminary tests show that the required penetration can consistently be achieved.

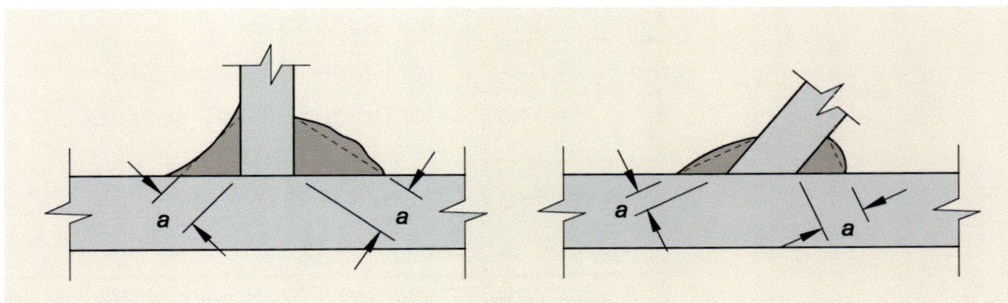

Figure 8.6 Throat thickness of a fillet weld

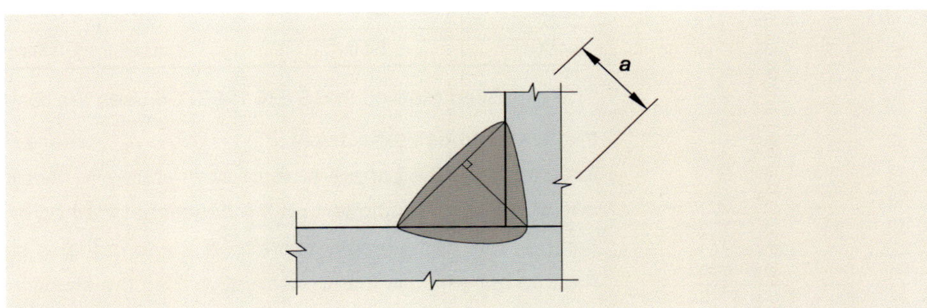

Figure 8.7 Throat thickness of a deep penetration fillet weld

8.3.3.3 Design resistance of fillet welds

4.5.3.1(1)

1. The design resistance of a fillet weld should be determined using the simplified method given below or the directional method, as given in 4.5.3.2 of BS EN 1993-1-8 or in accordance with below.

4.5.3.1(1)

2. The design resistance of a fillet weld may be assumed to be adequate if, at every point along its length, the resultant of all the forces per unit length transmitted by the weld satisfy the following criterion:

$$F_{w,Ed} \leq F_{w,Rd}$$

where:

$F_{w,Ed}$ is the design value of the weld force per unit length

$F_{w,Rd}$ is the design weld resistance per unit length.

4.5.3.3(2)

3. Independent of the orientation of the weld throat plane to the applied force, the design resistance per unit length $F_{w,Rd}$ should be determined from:

$$F_{w,Rd} = f_{vw,d}\, a$$

where:

$f_{vw,d}$ is the design shear strength of the weld.

4.5.3.3(3)

4. The design shear strength $f_{vw,d}$ of the weld should be determined from:

(4.4)

$$f_{vw,d} = \frac{f_u/\sqrt{3}}{\beta_w \gamma_{M2}}$$

where:

Table 4.1

f_u is the nominal ultimate tensile strength of the weaker part joined;

β_w $= 0.85$ for Grade S275

β_w $= 0.9$ for Grade S355

β_w $= 1.0$ for Grades S420 and S460

β_w $= 0.80$ for Grades HISTAR®460/460L[1]

The values given by expression (4.4) are:

Table 8.7 Design shear strength of fillet weld ($f_{vw,d}$)

Steel Grade	f_u (N/mm²)	Thickness of Weaker Jointed Part	$f_{vw,d}$ (N/mm²)
S275	410	$3\text{ mm} \le t_p \le 100\text{ mm}$	223
S355	470	$3\text{ mm} \le t_p \le 100\text{ mm}$	241
S460	540	$3\text{ mm} \le t_p \le 100\text{ mm}$	249

The simplified method in BS EN 1993-1-8 uses the resultant of the longitudinal and transverse forces (effectively $F_{w,Rd} = \sqrt{P_T^2 + P_L^2}$, where P_L is the longitudinal design force and P_T is the transverse force at an angle θ to the throat, see Figure 8.8). Hendy and Murphy[2] have shown that the directional method in 4.3.5.2 of BS EN 1993-1-8 can be more conveniently expressed in a form that is similar to that of the simplified method but which is less conservative than the simplified method. When there is no transverse force, the expression is the same as that for the simplified method in the Standard. This form of the directional method is given below.

5. As an alternative to the simplified method, the design resistance may be assumed to be adequate if the following criteria are satisfied:

$$\left(\frac{P_T^2}{K^2} + P_L^2\right)^{0.5} \le a f_{vw,d}$$

$$P_T \sin\theta \le \frac{a f_u}{\gamma_{M2}}$$

where:

P_T is the design value of the transverse force at an angle θ to the throat

P_L is the design value of the longitudinal design force

K $= \sqrt{\dfrac{3}{1 + 2\cos^2\theta}}$

1 ETA-10/0156.

2 Designers' guide to EN 1993-2, ICE Publishing, 2007.

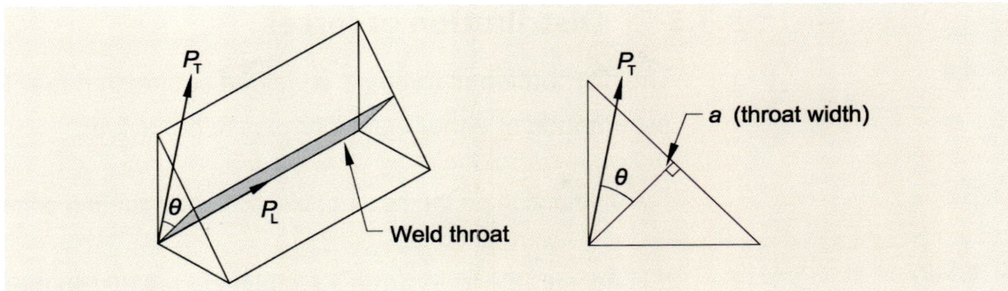

Figure 8.8 Notation for fillet welds

8.3.4 Design resistance of butt welds

8.3.4.1 Full penetration butt welds

4.7.1(1)

1. The design resistance of a full penetration butt weld should be taken as equal to the design resistance of the weaker of the parts connected, provided that the weld is made with a suitable consumable which will produce all-weld tensile specimens having both a minimum yield strength and a minimum tensile strength not less than those specified for the parent metal.

8.3.4.2 Partial penetration butt welds

4.7.2(1)

1. The design resistance of a partial penetration butt weld should be determined using the method for a deep penetration fillet weld and the throat thickness given in 8.3.3.

8.3.4.3 T-butt joints

4.5.3.2

4.7.3(1)

1. The design resistance of a T-butt joint, consisting of a pair of partial penetration butt welds reinforced by superimposed fillet welds, may be determined as for a full penetration butt weld if the total nominal throat thickness, exclusive of the unwelded gap, is not less than the thickness t of the part forming the stem of the tee joint, provided that the unwelded gap is not more than $(t/5)$ or 3 mm, whichever is less, see Figure 8.9.

4.7.3(2)

2. The design resistance of a T-butt joint which does not meet the requirements given above should be determined using the method for a fillet weld or a deep penetration fillet weld given in 8.3.3 depending on the amount of penetration. The throat thickness should be determined in conformity with the provisions for fillet welds or partial penetration butt welds as relevant.

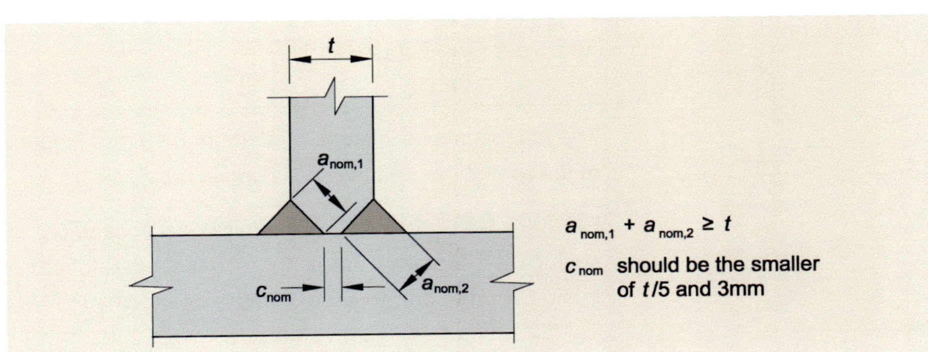

Figure 8.9 Effective full penetration of T-butt welds

8.3.5 Distribution of forces

4.9

1. The distribution of forces in a welded connection may be calculated on the assumption of either elastic or plastic behaviour.

> A distribution on the basis of elastic behaviour is recommended.

4.9(2)

2. It is acceptable to assume a simplified load distribution within the welds.

4.9(3)

3. Residual stresses and stresses not subject to transfer of load need not be included when checking the resistance of a weld. This applies specifically to the normal stress parallel to the axis of the weld.

4.9(4)

4. Welded joints should be designed to have adequate deformation capacity. However, ductility of the welds should not be relied upon.

8.3.6 Connections to unstiffened flanges

4.10

> Connections to unstiffened flanges are covered in clause 4.10. An effective width must be calculated, and the web of the supporting member verified.

8.3.7 Long Joints

4.11

> Long welded joints are unlikely to occur in structures within the scope of this guide. If a lap joint is longer than 150 times the throat thickness the joint must be treated as a 'long joint', see BS EN 1993-1-8, 4.11.

8.3.8 Eccentrically loaded single fillet or single-sided partial penetration butt welds

4.12(1)

1. Local eccentricity should be avoided whenever possible.

Local eccentricity (relative to the line of action of the force to be resisted) will result from the following loading conditions:

- Where a bending moment transmitted about the longitudinal axis of the weld produces tension at the root of the weld (see Figure 8.10);
- Where a tensile force transmitted perpendicular to the longitudinal axis of the weld produces a bending moment, resulting in a tension force at the root of the weld (see Figure 8.11).

> The four situations illustrated in Figure 8.10 and Figure 8.11 show tension produced at the root of the weld, which is undesirable.
>
> EN 1993-1-8 Clause 4.12(2) permits local eccentricity to be taken into account in such cases. However this is not recommended for conventional building structures in the UK – the design should ideally be modified to avoid the situation.

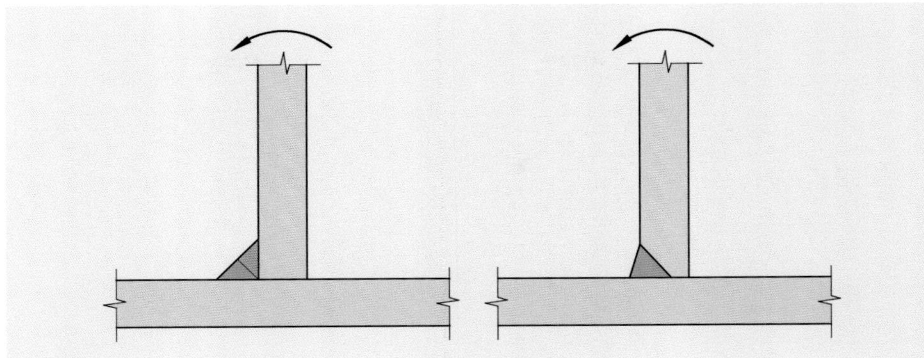

Figure 8.10 *Eccentric loading due to bending moment*

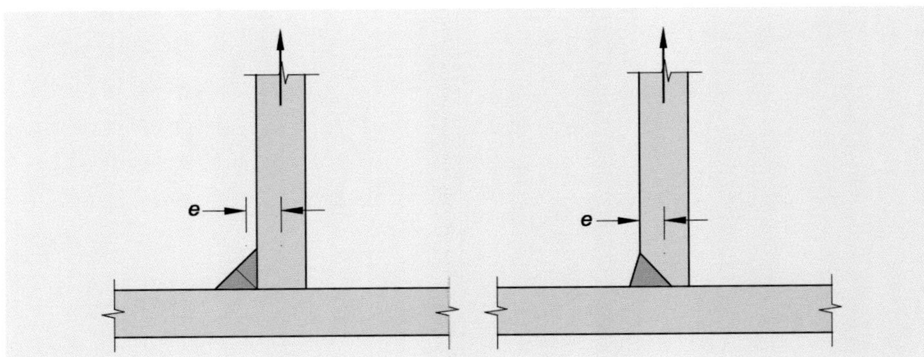

Figure 8.11 *Eccentric loading due to tensile force*

Simple connections

The design of beam-to-column connections in nominally pinned joints, column splices and nominally pinned column bases, all in accordance with BS EN 1993-1-8, is covered in *Joints in steel construction: Simple joints to Eurocode 3* (SCI publication P358). This publication also covers the resistance of connections to tying forces.

Moment Connections

The design of moment resisting connections in rigid and semi-rigid joints is covered in *Joints in steel construction: Moment resisting joints to Eurocode 3* (SCI publication P398). Although that publication does not adopt the same nomenclature, the basic design process accords closely with the process described in BS EN 1993-1-8.

APPENDIX A: DESIGN PROCEDURES

The following procedures all comply with the rules in the Eurocodes Parts and their National Annexes. Where reference to NCCI is necessary, the step is shaded.

A.1 Simply supported beam of rolled I or H cross-section

	Step	Reference in this publication	Reference in BS EN 1993-1-1
1	Establish support conditions and points of lateral restraint to compression flange.		
2	For ultimate limit state determine the maximum design shear forces V_{Ed} and moments M_{Ed} for the relevant actions using partial factors γ_F.	2.3.3	
3	Select trial beam size and steel grade.		
4	Classify its cross-section in bending.	Table 5.1	Table 5.2
5	Evaluate the full moment resistance of the cross-section and verify that $M_{Ed} \leq M_{c,Rd}$.	6.2.5	6.2.5
6	Evaluate the shear resistance of the cross-section $V_{pl,Rd}$. (Confirm that shear buckling is avoided).	6.2.6	6.2.6
7	If $V_{Ed} > V_{pl,Rd}$ then select a stronger section (thicker web)		
8	If $V_{Ed} > 0.5\,V_{pl,Rd}$ then determine the reduced resistance moment of the cross-section due to shear $M_{v,y,Rd}$ and verify that $M_{Ed} \leq M_{v,y,Rd}$	6.2.7	6.2.8
9	See whether resistance to lateral torsional buckling needs to be verified. If not (i.e. the compression flange is laterally restrained), go to (14).	6.3.2	6.3.2.1(2)
10	Determine non-dimensional slenderness $\bar{\lambda}_{LT}$.	6.3.2	6.3.2.2
11	If $\bar{\lambda}_{LT} \leq 0.4$ go to (14).		6.3.2.2(4)
12	Determine factor h/b and select appropriate value of χ_{LT} based on $\bar{\lambda}_{LT}$.	Table 6.6	Table 6.5 and NA6.3.2.3
	As an alternative to steps 10 – 12: i. Select the appropriate buckling curve ii. Calculate h/t_f iii. Calculate slenderness L/i_z iv. Choose the appropriate Table from Appendix E and determine χ_{LT}	Table 6.6	

	Step	Reference in this publication	Reference in BS EN 1993-1-1
13	Determine buckling resistance $M_{b,Rd}$ of member between lateral restraints. If $M_{b,Rd} > M_{Ed}$ the section is satisfactory. If not, select a stronger section. Repeat 9 to 13 between other points of lateral restraint, if necessary.	6.3.2	6.3.2.1
14	Using the characteristic combination of actions determine the maximum vertical deflection of the beam under variable actions only.	2.3.5	
15	Verify that the vertical deflection satisfies the Client's requirements	7.2.1	
16	Consider dynamic effects, where appropriate.		
17	Select appropriate steel sub-grade	4.1.2	

A.2 Tension members

	Step	Reference in this publication	Reference in BS EN 1993-1-1
1	For the ultimate limit state, determine the design axial force N_{Ed} for the relevant actions, using partial safety factors γ_F.	2.3.3	
2	Select steel grade		
3	Select a trial member size and check thickness limitation for chosen quality. [As a first approximation, select a cross-section area that satisfies $N_{Ed}/A < f_y$.]		
4	Determine the design tension resistance ($N_{t,Rd}$). For sections with holes $N_{t,Rd}$ should be taken as the smaller of $N_{pl,Rd}$ and $N_{u,Rd}$. For sections without holes $N_{t,Rd} = N_{pl,Rd}$.	6.2.3	6.2.3
5	If $N_{Ed}/N_{t,Rd} \leq 1.0$ the section is satisfactory		6.2.3(1)
6	Select appropriate steel sub-grade.	4.1.2	

A.3 Compression members

	Step	Reference in this publication	Reference in BS EN 1993-1-1
1	For the ultimate limit state, determine the design compressive force N_{Ed} for the relevant load case, using partial safety factors γ_F.	2.3.3	
2	Select steel grade		
3	Select a trial column size and check thickness limitation for chosen quality. [As a first approximation, select a cross-section area that satisfies $N_{Ed}/A < f_y$.]		
4	Classify cross-section. If cross-section is class 4, see EN 1993-1-5 or chose a thicker cross-section	Table 5.1	Table 5.2
5	Determine the buckling length L_{cr} for each axis.	6.3.1	
6	Determine the non-dimensional slenderness $\bar{\lambda}$ for each axis	6.3.1	6.3.1.3(1)
7	Select the appropriate buckling curve for each axis, for the type of cross-section and thickness of steel	Table 6.2	Table 6.2
8	For each axis, determine the flexural buckling reduction factor, χ and adopt the lower value	Table 6.3	6.3.1.2
9	Determine the buckling resistance $N_{b,Rd}$. If $N_{b,Rd} > N_{Ed}$ the selected section is satisfactory	6.3.1	6.3.1.1(3)
10	Select appropriate steel sub-grade	4.1.2	

A.4 Compression members with moment

	Step	Reference in this publication	Reference in BS EN 1993-1-1
1	Determine $N_{b,y,Rd}$ and $N_{b,z,Rd}$ (see A.3).	6.3.1	6.3.1.1(3)
2	Determine $M_{b,R}$ (see A.1).	6.3.2	6.3.2
3	Determine $M_{cb,z,Rd}$ (see note).	6.2.5	6.2.5
4	Determine C_{my}, C_{mz} and C_{mLT} based on the shape of the bending moment diagrams	Table D.2	Table B.3
5	Based on section type and cross-section classification, select appropriate figures for evaluation of k factors	Table D.1	
6	Determine k factors based on $\bar{\lambda}$ and $N_{Ed} / N_{b,Rd}$ using the appropriate figures.	6.3.3 and Appendix D	Table B.1 or Table B.2
7	Verify for biaxial bending combined with flexural buckling about the major axis using: $\frac{N_{Ed}}{N_{b,y,Rd}} + k_{yy}\frac{M_{y,Ed}}{M_{b,Rd}} + k_{yz}\frac{M_{z,Ed}}{M_{c,z,Rd}} \leq 1$ If this is not satisfied, choose a stronger section.	6.3.3	6.3.3(4)
8	Verify for biaxial bending combined with flexural buckling about the minor axis using: $\frac{N_{Ed}}{N_{b,z,Rd}} + k_{zy}\frac{M_{y,Ed}}{M_{b,Rd}} + k_{zz}\frac{M_{z,Ed}}{M_{c,z,Rd}} \leq 1$ If this is not satisfied, choose a stronger section.	6.3.3	6.3.3(4)

Notes:
$M_{c,z,Rd}$ is given by $M_{c,z,Rd} = \frac{f_y W_z}{\gamma_{M1}}$, which is the same as the design value of the bending resistance of the cross-section in the minor axis as given in 6.2.5 when $\gamma_{M1} = \gamma_{M0}$
See A.5 for a simplified approach for columns in simple construction.
For members that are not susceptible to lateral torsional buckling, where the member is subject to compression and major axis bending only (i.e. $M_{z,Ed} = 0$), k_{zy} may be taken as $k_{zy} = 0$

A.5 Columns in simple construction

	Step	Reference in this publication	Reference in BS EN 1993-1-1
1	For the ultimate limit state, determine the design compressive force N_{Ed} for the relevant actions, using partial factors γ_F and ψ_i.	2.3.3	
2	Select steel grade and quality.		
3	Select a trial column size and check thickness limitation for chosen quality. [As a first approximation, select a cross-section area that satisfies $N_{Ed}/A < f_y$.].		
4	Classify cross-section in compression. If cross-section is Class 4 chose a thicker cross-section.	Table 5.1	Table 5.2
5	Determine the buckling length L_{cr} for each axis.	6.3.1	
6	Determine the design buckling resistance for each axis ($N_{b,y,Rd}$ and $N_{b,z,Rd}$).	6.3.1	6.3.1.1(3)
7	Select the minimum buckling resistance $N_{min,b,Rd}$.		
8	For the ultimate limit state. determine the design bending moments $M_{y,Ed}$ and $M_{z,Ed}$ for the relevant load case, using partial factors γ_F and combination factors ψ_i. An eccentricity of 100 mm from the connection should be considered when determining these moments.		
9	Verify that the criteria given in 6.3.4 are satisfied. If the criteria are not satisfied the design steps given in Appendix A.4 should be followed.	6.3.4	
10	Determine $N_{min,b,Rd}$.	6.3.1	
11	Determine $\bar{\lambda}_{LT}$.	6.3.2	6.3.2.2(1)
12	Determine χ_{LT}.	6.3.2	6.3.2.3(1)
13	Determine $M_{b,Rd}$.	6.3.2	
14	Determine $M_{c,z,Rd}$ $M_{c,z,Rd}$ is the cross-sectional bending resistance in the minor axis, when $\gamma_{M1} = \gamma_{M0}$.	6.2.5	
15	Verify that: $\frac{N_{Ed}}{N_{min,b,Rd}} + \frac{M_{y,Ed}}{M_{b,Rd}} + 1.5\frac{M_{z,Ed}}{M_{c,z,Rd}} \leq 1$ If the above verification is not satisfied, select a larger section.	6.3.4	

APPENDIX B: COMMON SYMBOLS

B.1 Dimensions

b width of a cross-section

h depth of a cross-section

d depth of straight portion of a web, nominal diameter of a bolt

t_w web thickness

t_f flange thickness

t thickness

d_0 diameter of hole for a bolt

a effective throat thickness for a fillet weld.

B.2 Material properties

f_y yield strength

f_u ultimate strength

E modulus of elasticity

G shear modulus

ν Poisson's ratio in elastic stage

ε coefficient depending on f_y.

B.3 Geometric parameters of cross-section

A_{eff} effective area of a cross-section

A_w area of a web

A_f area of one flange

I second moment of area

W_{pl} plastic section modulus

$W_{el,min}$ minimum elastic section modulus

$W_{eff,min}$ minimum effective section modulus

i radius of gyration about the relevant axis, determined using the properties of the gross cross-section.

B.4 Parameters for members

$\bar{\lambda}$	non-dimensional slenderness
$\bar{\lambda}_{LT}$	non-dimensional slenderness for lateral-torsional buckling
χ	reduction factor for the relevant buckling curve
χ_{LT}	reduction factor for lateral-torsional buckling
N_{cr}	elastic critical force for the relevant buckling mode based on the gross cross sectional properties
M_{cr}	elastic critical moment for lateral-torsional buckling.

B.5 Effects of actions

N_{Ed}	design normal force
$M_{y,Ed}$	design bending moment, y-y axis
$M_{z,Ed}$	design bending moment, z-z axis
M_{Ed}	design bending moment
V_{Ed}	design shear force
L_{c}	length between lateral restraints.

B.6 Resistances of sections, members and elements

Symbols for resistance of cross-sections

$N_{t,Rd}$	design value of the resistance to tension forces
$N_{pl,Rd}$	design plastic resistance to normal forces of the gross cross-section
$N_{u,Rd}$	design ultimate resistance to normal forces of the net cross-section at holes for fasteners
$N_{c,Rd}$	design resistance to normal forces of the cross-section for uniform compression
$M_{c,Rd}$	design resistance for bending about one principal axis of a cross-section (thus $M_{c,y,Rd}$; $M_{c,z,Rd}$)
$V_{c,Rd}$	design shear resistance
$V_{pl,Rd}$	plastic design shear resistance.

Symbols for resistance of members

$M_{b,Rd}$	design buckling resistance moment.

Symbols for resistance of fasteners

$F_{b,Rd}$	design bearing resistance per bolt
$F_{t,Rd}$	design tension resistance per bolt
$F_{v,Rd}$	design shear resistance per bolt.

B.7 Utilisation factors

α_{cr} factor by which the design loads would have to be increased to cause elastic instability in a global mode.

B.8 Partial factors on resistance

γ_{M0} partial factor for resistance of cross-sections whatever the Class is

γ_{M1} partial factor for resistance of members to instability assessed by member checks

γ_{M2} partial factor for resistance of cross-sections in tension to fracture.

APPENDIX C: COMBINATION FACTORS

Table C.1 Partiall, combination and reduction factors for the STR and GEO ultimate limit states for buildings in the UK

Expression	Unfavourable permanent actions			Unfavourable variable actions*					
	Self-weight			Imposed floor loads			Wind actions or snow loads		
6.10	$\gamma_{Gj,sup}$	= 1.35		$\gamma_{Q,1}$	= 1.5		$\gamma_{Q,i}\ \psi_{0,i}$	= 1.5 × 0.5	= 0.75
	$\gamma_{Gj,sup}$	= 1.35		$\gamma_{Q,i}\ \psi_{0,i}$	= 1.5 × 0.7	= 1.05	$\gamma_{Q,1}$	= 1.5	
6.10a +	$\gamma_{Gj,sup}$	= 1.35		$\boldsymbol{\gamma_{Q,1}\ \psi_{0,1}}$	**= 1.5 × 0.7**	**= 1.05**	$\gamma_{Q,i}\ \psi_{0,i}$	= 1.5 × 0.5	= 0.75
	$\gamma_{Gj,sup}$	= 1.35		$\gamma_{Q,i}\ \psi_{0,i}$	= 1.5 × 0.7	= 1.05	$\boldsymbol{\gamma_{Q,1}\ \psi_{0,1}}$	**= 1.5 × 0.5**	**= 0.75**
6.10b	$\xi\gamma_{Gj,sup}$	= 0.925 × 1.35	= 1.25	$\gamma_{Q,1}$	= 1.5		$\gamma_{Q,i}\ \psi_{0,i}$	= 1.5 × 0.5	= 0.75
	$\xi\gamma_{Gj,sup}$	= 0.925 × 1.35	= 1.25	$\gamma_{Q,i}\ \psi_{0,i}$	= 1.5 × 0.7	= 1.05	$\gamma_{Q,1}$	= 1.5	

Notes:

All factor values given above are taken from the National Annex to BS EN 1990.

Shaded boxes indicate the '*leading variable action*'.

Bold text indicates the '*main accompanying variable action*'.

The remaining variable actions are the '*other accompanying variable actions*'.

\+ The same values are obtained for each of the three variations of expression (6.10a) (i.e. when each variable action in turn is treated as the main accompanying action) because the UK National Annex specifies the same value for $\gamma_{Q,1}$ and $\gamma_{Q,i}$.

* For snow loads $\psi_{0,1}$ and $\psi_{0,i}$ values are for buildings at an altitude of less than 1000 m above mean sea level.

APPENDIX D: INTERACTION FACTORS

Table D.1 Interaction factors for combined axial compression and bending

Interaction factors	Criteria	Section type	Section Class 1 and 2	Section Class 3	C Factor
k_{yy}	-	All	Figure D.2	Figure D.3	C_{my}
k_{yz}	-	All	$0.6\ k_{zz}$	k_{zz}	-
k_{zz}	Member not susceptible to torsional deformation	RHS sections	Figure D.7	Figure D.8	C_{mz}
	Member susceptible to torsional deformation	I sections	Figure D.6	Figure D.8	C_{mz}
k_{zy}	Member not susceptible to torsional deformation	All	$0.6\ k_{yy}$	$0.8\ k_{yy}$	-
	Member susceptible to torsional deformation	All	Figure D.4	Figure D.5	C_{mLT}

[1] C Factors may be obtained from Table D.2

[2] In Figure D.4 and Figure D.5, k_{zy} is based on the conservative assumption that $C_{mLT} = 1.0$.

Table D.2 Equivalent uniform moment factors C_m in Table D.1

Moment Diagram	Range		C_{my}, C_{mz} and $C_{m,LT}$ Uniform Loading	C_{my}, C_{mz} and $C_{m,LT}$ Concentrated Load
Linear moment 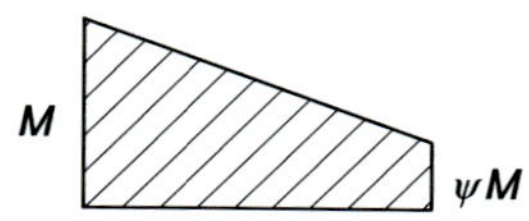	$-1 \le \psi \le 1$		$0.6 + 0.4\psi \ge 0.4$	
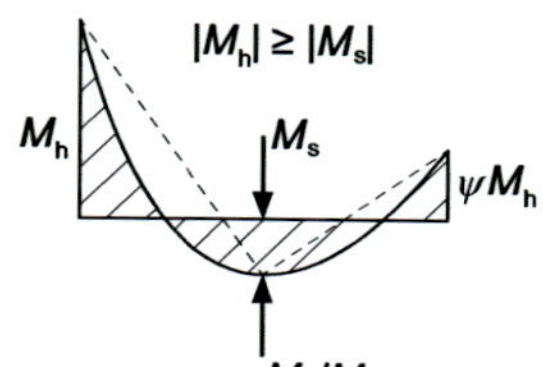	$0 \le \alpha_s \le 1$	$-1 \le \psi \le 1$	$0.2 + 0.8\,\alpha_s \ge 0.4$	$0.2 + 0.8\,\alpha_s \ge 0.4$
	$-1 \le \alpha_s < 0$	$0 \le \psi \le 1$	$0.1 - 0.8\,\alpha_s \ge 0.4$	$-0.8\,\alpha_s \ge 0.4$
		$-1 \le \psi < 0$	$0.1(1-\psi) - 0.8\,\alpha_s \ge 0.4$	$0.2(-\psi) - 0.8\,\alpha_s \ge 0.4$
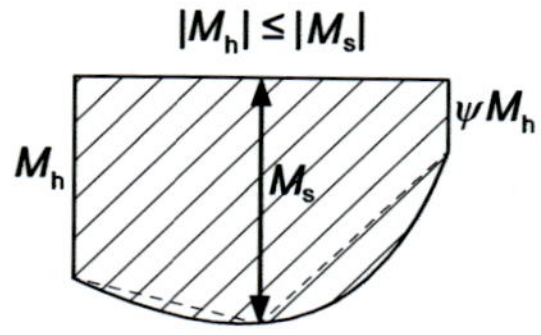	$0 \le \alpha_h \le 1$	$-1 \le \psi \le 1$	$0.95 + 0.05\,\alpha_h$	$0.90 + 0.10\,\alpha_h$
	$-1 \le \alpha_h < 0$	$0 \le \psi \le 1$	$0.95 + 0.05\,\alpha_h$	$0.90 + 0.10\,\alpha_h$
		$-1 \le \psi < 0$	$0.95 + 0.05\,\alpha_h(1+2\psi)$	$0.90 + 0.10\,\alpha_h(1+2\psi)$

For members with sway buckling mode the equivalent uniform moment factor should be taken $C_{my} = 0.9$ or $C_{mz} = 0.9$ respectively.

C_{my}, C_{mz} and C_{mLT} should be obtained according to the bending moment diagram between the relevant braced points as follows:

Moment factor	Bending axis	Points braced in direction
C_{my}	y-y	z-z
C_{mz}	z-z	y-y
C_{mLT}	y-y	y-y

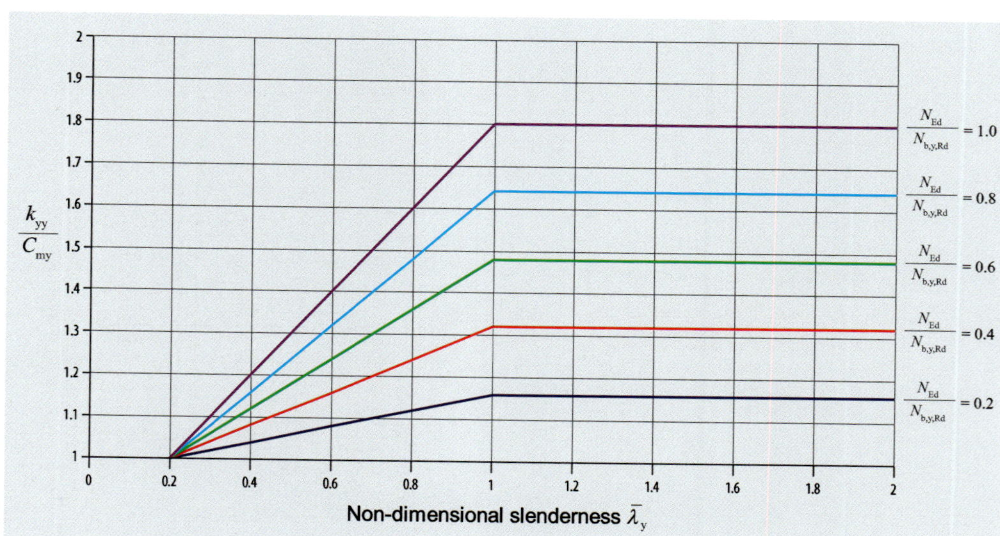

Figure D.1 Interaction factor k_{yy} for Class 1 and 2 sections

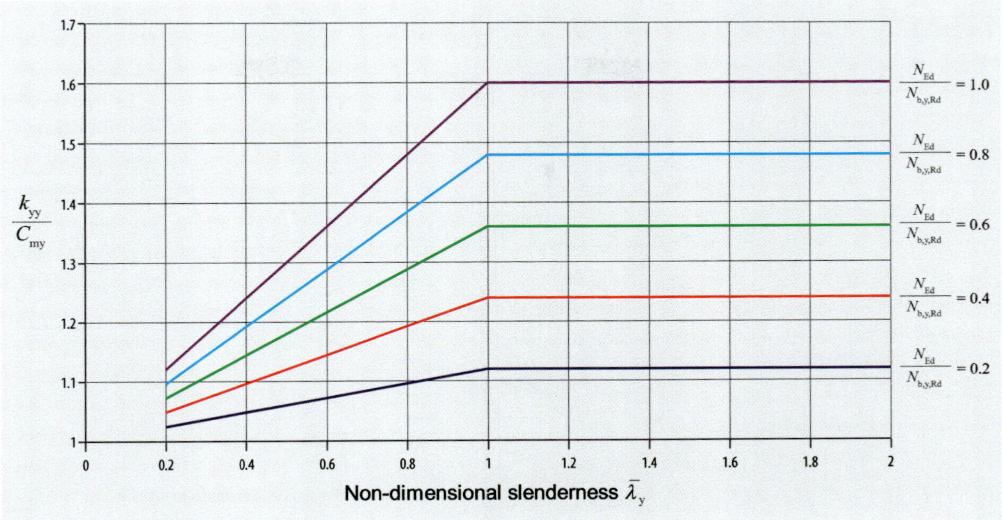

Figure D.2 *Interaction factors k_y for Class 3 sections*

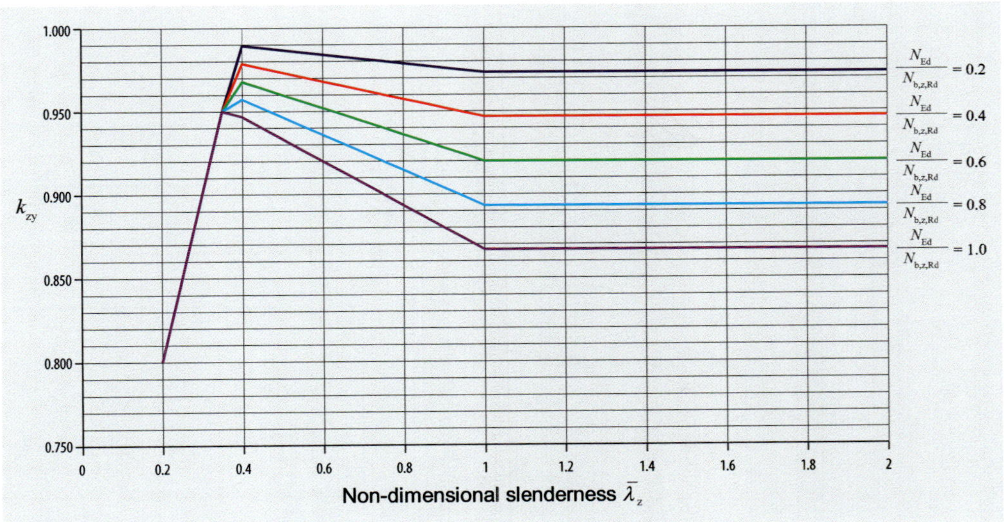

Figure D.3 *Interaction factors k_{zy} for $C_{mLT} = 1.0$, Class 1 and 2 I sections*

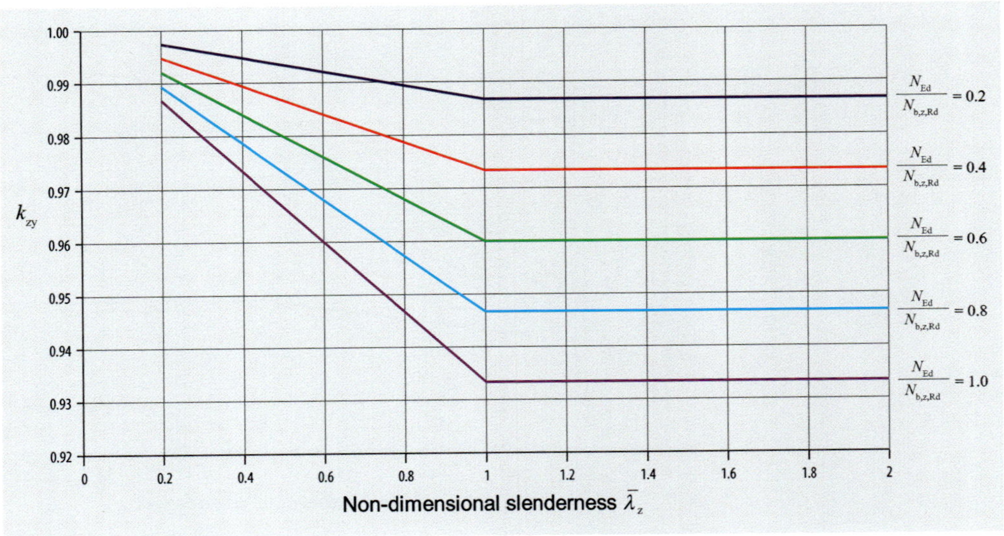

Figure D.4 *Interaction factors k_{zy} for $C_{mLT} = 1.0$, Class 3 I sections*

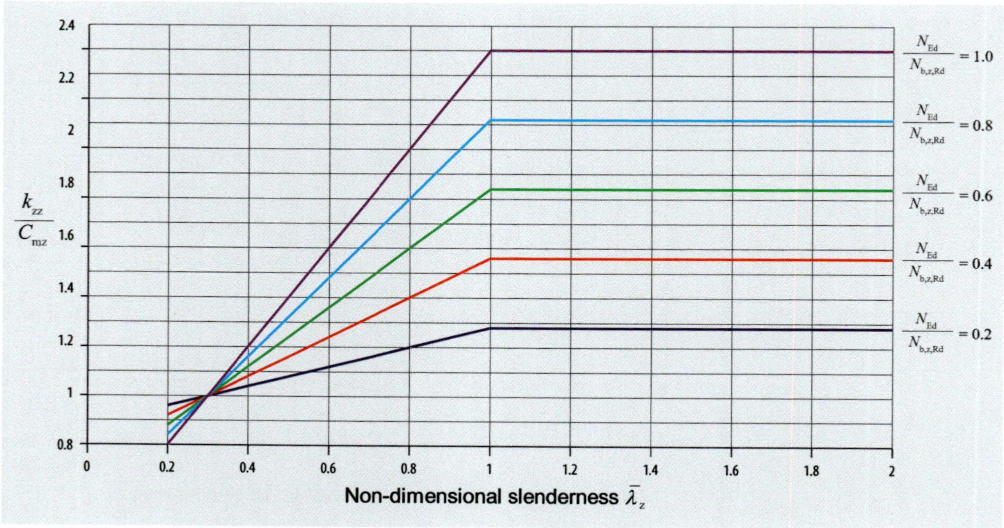

Figure D.5 *Interaction factors k_{zz} for Class 1 and 2 I sections*

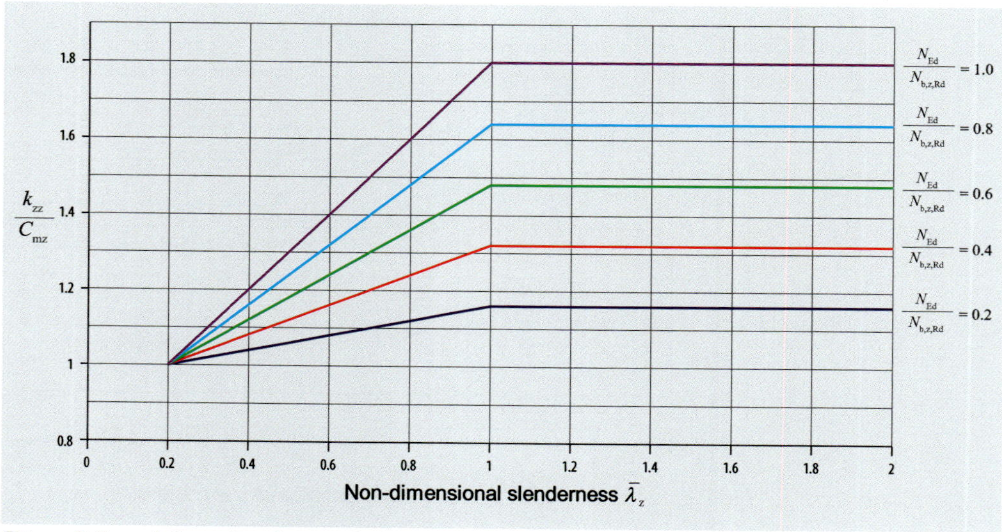

Figure D.6 *Interaction factors k_{zz} for Class 1 and 2 RHS sections*

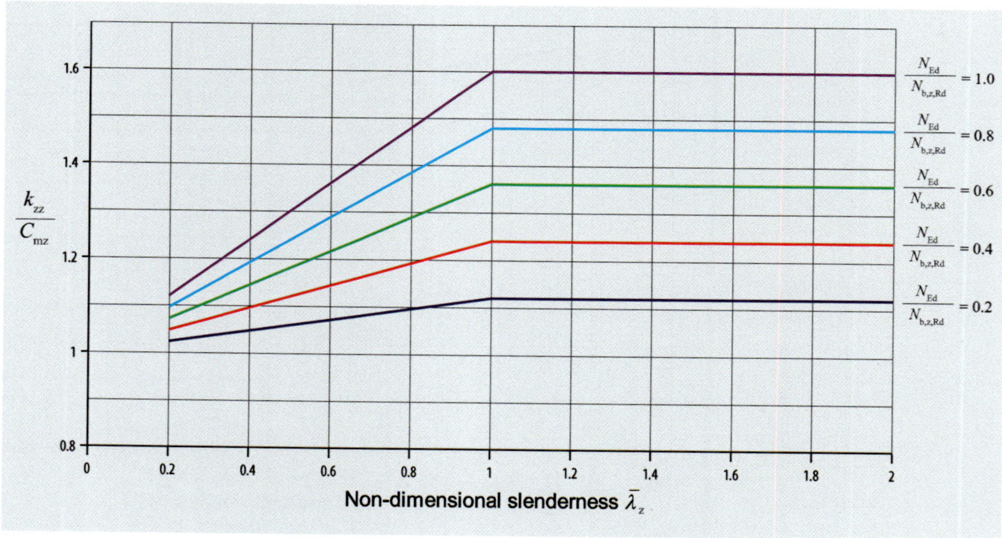

Figure D.7 *Interaction factors k_{zz} for Class 3 I sections and RHS sections*

APPENDIX E: REDUCTION FACTOR FOR LTB RESISTANCE - TABULAR EVALUATION

As explained in 6.3.2, the non-dimensional slenderness $\bar{\lambda}_{LT}$ may be based on the expression:

$$\bar{\lambda}_{LT} = \frac{1}{\sqrt{C_1}} UV\bar{\lambda}_z\sqrt{\beta_w}$$ and then χ_{LT} may be calculated.

Based on this expression, χ_{LT} may be related to the slenderness L/i_z and the section property h/t_f.

The following tables may be used to determine χ_{LT}, based on the following:

1. $C_1 = 1$. This may be very conservative when the bending moment is not uniform.
2. $\beta_w = 1$. This is conservative for Class 3 sections.
3. $U = 0.9$.
4. The tables assume a design strength based on a maximum thickness of 16 mm. This is slightly conservative if the elements are greater than 16 mm (Note that in all cases the correct design strength should be used when calculating the product $\chi_{LT} \times f_y \times W_y$ (e.g. use 275 N/mm^2, 265 N/mm^2, 255 N/mm^2 as appropriate).
5. The tables presume that the moment resistance need not be reduced due to shear – i.e. that the applied shear is less than 50% of the shear resistance.
6. Tables are provided for S275, S355 and S460, for
   - Buckling curve b for sections where $h/b \leq 2$
   - Buckling curve c for sections where $2 < h/b \leq 3.1$

Additional guidance, for sections outside these ranges, may be found in *Steel building design: Design Data* 'the Blue Book' (SCI publication P363) and the 'Orange Book' at http://orangebook.arcelormittal.com.

Table E.1 χ_{LT} for S275, Curve b, $h/b \leq 2$

$\lambda_z = L/i_z$	$\bar{\lambda}_z$	h/t_f									
		5	10	15	20	25	30	35	40	45	50
30	0.35	1.00	1.00	1.00	1.00	1.00	1.00	1.00	1.00	1.00	1.00
40	0.46	1.00	1.00	1.00	1.00	1.00	1.00	1.00	1.00	1.00	1.00
50	0.58	1.00	0.99	0.97	0.97	0.96	0.96	0.96	0.96	0.96	0.96
60	0.69	1.00	0.97	0.94	0.93	0.92	0.92	0.92	0.91	0.91	0.91
70	0.81	1.00	0.95	0.92	0.90	0.89	0.88	0.87	0.87	0.87	0.87
80	0.92	0.99	0.93	0.89	0.86	0.85	0.83	0.83	0.82	0.82	0.81
90	1.04	0.98	0.91	0.86	0.83	0.80	0.79	0.78	0.77	0.77	0.76
100	1.15	0.97	0.89	0.83	0.79	0.76	0.74	0.73	0.72	0.71	0.71
110	1.27	0.96	0.87	0.80	0.76	0.72	0.70	0.68	0.67	0.66	0.65
120	1.38	0.95	0.85	0.78	0.72	0.68	0.65	0.63	0.62	0.61	0.60
130	1.50	0.94	0.83	0.75	0.69	0.65	0.61	0.59	0.57	0.56	0.55
140	1.61	0.93	0.82	0.73	0.66	0.61	0.58	0.55	0.53	0.52	0.50
150	1.73	0.92	0.80	0.70	0.63	0.58	0.54	0.51	0.49	0.48	0.46
160	1.84	0.91	0.78	0.68	0.60	0.55	0.51	0.48	0.46	0.44	0.43
170	1.96	0.90	0.77	0.66	0.58	0.52	0.48	0.45	0.43	0.41	0.40
180	2.07	0.89	0.75	0.64	0.55	0.49	0.45	0.42	0.40	0.38	0.37
190	2.19	0.88	0.73	0.62	0.53	0.47	0.43	0.40	0.38	0.36	0.34
200	2.30	0.87	0.72	0.60	0.51	0.45	0.41	0.38	0.35	0.34	0.32
210	2.42	0.87	0.70	0.58	0.49	0.43	0.39	0.36	0.33	0.32	0.30
220	2.53	0.86	0.69	0.56	0.47	0.41	0.37	0.34	0.32	0.30	0.29
230	2.65	0.85	0.67	0.54	0.46	0.40	0.35	0.32	0.30	0.28	0.27
240	2.76	0.84	0.66	0.53	0.44	0.38	0.34	0.31	0.29	0.27	0.26
250	2.88	0.83	0.65	0.51	0.43	0.37	0.32	0.29	0.27	0.26	0.24

Table E.2 χ_{LT} for S275, Curve c, $2 < h/b \leq 3.1$

$\lambda_z = L/i_z$	$\bar{\lambda}_z$	h/t_f									
		5	**10**	**15**	**20**	**25**	**30**	**35**	**40**	**45**	**50**
30	0.35	1.00	1.00	1.00	1.00	1.00	1.00	1.00	1.00	1.00	1.00
40	0.46	1.00	1.00	1.00	1.00	1.00	1.00	1.00	0.99	0.99	0.99
50	0.58	1.00	0.99	0.96	0.95	0.95	0.94	0.94	0.94	0.94	0.94
60	0.69	1.00	0.95	0.92	0.91	0.90	0.89	0.89	0.88	0.88	0.88
70	0.81	1.00	0.93	0.88	0.86	0.85	0.84	0.83	0.83	0.82	0.82
80	0.92	0.98	0.90	0.85	0.82	0.80	0.78	0.77	0.77	0.76	0.76
90	1.04	0.97	0.87	0.81	0.77	0.75	0.73	0.72	0.71	0.71	0.70
100	1.15	0.95	0.85	0.78	0.73	0.70	0.68	0.67	0.66	0.65	0.64
110	1.27	0.94	0.83	0.75	0.70	0.66	0.64	0.62	0.61	0.60	0.59
120	1.38	0.93	0.80	0.72	0.66	0.62	0.60	0.58	0.56	0.55	0.54
130	1.50	0.91	0.78	0.69	0.63	0.59	0.56	0.53	0.52	0.51	0.50
140	1.61	0.90	0.76	0.67	0.60	0.55	0.52	0.50	0.48	0.47	0.46
150	1.73	0.89	0.74	0.64	0.57	0.52	0.49	0.46	0.45	0.43	0.42
160	1.84	0.88	0.73	0.62	0.55	0.50	0.46	0.43	0.42	0.40	0.39
170	1.96	0.86	0.71	0.60	0.52	0.47	0.43	0.41	0.39	0.37	0.36
180	2.07	0.85	0.69	0.58	0.50	0.45	0.41	0.38	0.36	0.35	0.34
190	2.19	0.84	0.67	0.56	0.48	0.43	0.39	0.36	0.34	0.33	0.32
200	2.30	0.83	0.66	0.54	0.46	0.41	0.37	0.34	0.32	0.31	0.30
210	2.42	0.82	0.64	0.52	0.45	0.39	0.35	0.33	0.31	0.29	0.28
220	2.53	0.81	0.63	0.51	0.43	0.38	0.34	0.31	0.29	0.28	0.26
230	2.65	0.80	0.61	0.49	0.41	0.36	0.32	0.30	0.28	0.26	0.25
240	2.76	0.79	0.60	0.48	0.40	0.35	0.31	0.28	0.26	0.25	0.24
250	2.88	0.78	0.59	0.47	0.39	0.34	0.30	0.27	0.25	0.24	0.23

Table E.3 χ_{LT} *for S355, Curve b,* $h/b \leq 2$

$\lambda_z = L/i_z$	$\bar{\lambda}_z$	h/t_f									
		5	**10**	**15**	**20**	**25**	**30**	**35**	**40**	**45**	**50**
30	0.39	1.00	1.00	1.00	1.00	1.00	1.00	1.00	1.00	1.00	1.00
40	0.52	1.00	1.00	0.99	0.98	0.98	0.98	0.97	0.97	0.97	0.97
50	0.65	1.00	0.97	0.95	0.94	0.93	0.93	0.93	0.93	0.93	0.93
60	0.79	0.99	0.94	0.91	0.90	0.89	0.88	0.88	0.88	0.87	0.87
70	0.92	0.98	0.91	0.88	0.85	0.84	0.83	0.82	0.82	0.82	0.81
80	1.05	0.96	0.89	0.84	0.81	0.79	0.78	0.77	0.76	0.76	0.75
90	1.18	0.95	0.87	0.81	0.77	0.74	0.72	0.71	0.70	0.69	0.69
100	1.31	0.94	0.84	0.77	0.72	0.69	0.67	0.65	0.64	0.63	0.62
110	1.44	0.93	0.82	0.74	0.68	0.64	0.61	0.60	0.58	0.57	0.56
120	1.57	0.91	0.80	0.71	0.64	0.60	0.57	0.55	0.53	0.52	0.51
130	1.70	0.90	0.78	0.68	0.61	0.56	0.52	0.50	0.48	0.47	0.46
140	1.83	0.89	0.75	0.65	0.57	0.52	0.49	0.46	0.44	0.43	0.42
150	1.96	0.88	0.73	0.62	0.54	0.49	0.45	0.43	0.41	0.39	0.38
160	2.09	0.87	0.71	0.60	0.51	0.46	0.42	0.40	0.38	0.36	0.35
170	2.23	0.86	0.69	0.57	0.49	0.43	0.40	0.37	0.35	0.33	0.32
180	2.36	0.85	0.67	0.55	0.47	0.41	0.37	0.35	0.33	0.31	0.30
190	2.49	0.84	0.66	0.53	0.44	0.39	0.35	0.32	0.30	0.29	0.28
200	2.62	0.83	0.64	0.51	0.43	0.37	0.33	0.31	0.29	0.27	0.26
210	2.75	0.81	0.62	0.49	0.41	0.35	0.32	0.29	0.27	0.25	0.24
220	2.88	0.80	0.60	0.47	0.39	0.34	0.30	0.27	0.25	0.24	0.23
230	3.01	0.79	0.59	0.46	0.38	0.32	0.29	0.26	0.24	0.23	0.22
240	3.14	0.78	0.57	0.44	0.36	0.31	0.27	0.25	0.23	0.21	0.20
250	3.27	0.77	0.56	0.43	0.35	0.30	0.26	0.24	0.22	0.20	0.19

Table E.4 χ_{LT} *for S355, Curve c,* $2 < h/b \leq 3.1$

$\lambda_z = L/i_z$	$\bar{\lambda}_z$	h/t_f									
		5	**10**	**15**	**20**	**25**	**30**	**35**	**40**	**45**	**50**
30	0.39	1.00	1.00	1.00	1.00	1.00	1.00	1.00	1.00	1.00	1.00
40	0.52	1.00	1.00	0.98	0.97	0.97	0.97	0.96	0.96	0.96	0.96
50	0.65	1.00	0.95	0.93	0.91	0.91	0.90	0.90	0.90	0.90	0.90
60	0.79	0.99	0.92	0.88	0.86	0.85	0.84	0.84	0.83	0.83	0.83
70	0.92	0.97	0.88	0.83	0.81	0.79	0.78	0.77	0.77	0.76	0.76
80	1.05	0.95	0.85	0.79	0.76	0.73	0.72	0.71	0.70	0.70	0.69
90	1.18	0.93	0.82	0.75	0.71	0.68	0.66	0.65	0.64	0.63	0.63
100	1.31	0.91	0.79	0.71	0.66	0.63	0.61	0.59	0.58	0.57	0.57
110	1.44	0.90	0.77	0.68	0.62	0.58	0.56	0.54	0.53	0.52	0.51
120	1.57	0.88	0.74	0.65	0.58	0.54	0.51	0.49	0.48	0.47	0.46
130	1.70	0.87	0.72	0.62	0.55	0.51	0.48	0.45	0.44	0.43	0.42
140	1.83	0.85	0.69	0.59	0.52	0.47	0.44	0.42	0.40	0.39	0.38
150	1.96	0.84	0.67	0.56	0.49	0.44	0.41	0.39	0.37	0.36	0.35
160	2.09	0.83	0.65	0.54	0.47	0.42	0.39	0.36	0.34	0.33	0.32
170	2.23	0.81	0.63	0.52	0.44	0.40	0.36	0.34	0.32	0.31	0.30
180	2.36	0.80	0.61	0.50	0.42	0.37	0.34	0.32	0.30	0.29	0.28
190	2.49	0.79	0.60	0.48	0.40	0.36	0.32	0.30	0.28	0.27	0.26
200	2.62	0.77	0.58	0.46	0.39	0.34	0.31	0.28	0.26	0.25	0.24
210	2.75	0.76	0.56	0.44	0.37	0.32	0.29	0.27	0.25	0.24	0.23
220	2.88	0.75	0.55	0.43	0.36	0.31	0.28	0.25	0.24	0.22	0.21
230	3.01	0.74	0.53	0.42	0.34	0.30	0.26	0.24	0.22	0.21	0.20
240	3.14	0.73	0.52	0.40	0.33	0.28	0.25	0.23	0.21	0.20	0.19
250	3.27	0.71	0.51	0.39	0.32	0.27	0.24	0.22	0.20	0.19	0.18

Table E.5 χ_{LT} *for S460, Curve b,* $h/b \leq 2$

$\lambda_z = L/i_z$	$\bar{\lambda}_z$	h/t_f									
		5	10	15	20	25	30	35	40	45	50
30	0.45	1.00	1.00	1.00	1.00	1.00	1.00	1.00	1.00	1.00	1.00
40	0.60	1.00	0.98	0.96	0.96	0.95	0.95	0.95	0.95	0.95	0.95
50	0.74	0.99	0.94	0.92	0.91	0.90	0.89	0.89	0.89	0.89	0.89
60	0.89	0.97	0.91	0.87	0.85	0.84	0.83	0.83	0.83	0.82	0.82
70	1.04	0.95	0.88	0.83	0.80	0.78	0.77	0.76	0.76	0.75	0.75
80	1.19	0.94	0.84	0.78	0.74	0.72	0.70	0.69	0.68	0.68	0.67
90	1.34	0.92	0.81	0.74	0.69	0.66	0.64	0.62	0.61	0.61	0.60
100	1.49	0.91	0.79	0.70	0.64	0.60	0.58	0.56	0.55	0.54	0.53
110	1.64	0.89	0.76	0.66	0.60	0.55	0.53	0.51	0.49	0.48	0.47
120	1.79	0.88	0.73	0.62	0.55	0.51	0.48	0.46	0.44	0.43	0.42
130	1.94	0.86	0.70	0.59	0.52	0.47	0.44	0.42	0.40	0.39	0.38
140	2.09	0.85	0.68	0.56	0.48	0.43	0.40	0.38	0.36	0.35	0.34
150	2.23	0.83	0.65	0.53	0.45	0.40	0.37	0.35	0.33	0.32	0.31
160	2.38	0.82	0.63	0.51	0.43	0.38	0.34	0.32	0.30	0.29	0.28
170	2.53	0.80	0.61	0.48	0.40	0.35	0.32	0.30	0.28	0.27	0.26
180	2.68	0.79	0.59	0.46	0.38	0.33	0.30	0.28	0.26	0.25	0.24
190	2.83	0.78	0.57	0.44	0.36	0.32	0.28	0.26	0.24	0.23	0.22
200	2.98	0.76	0.55	0.42	0.35	0.30	0.27	0.24	0.23	0.22	0.21
210	3.13	0.75	0.53	0.41	0.33	0.28	0.25	0.23	0.21	0.20	0.19
220	3.28	0.74	0.51	0.39	0.32	0.27	0.24	0.22	0.20	0.19	0.18
230	3.43	0.72	0.50	0.37	0.30	0.26	0.23	0.21	0.19	0.18	0.17
240	3.58	0.71	0.48	0.36	0.29	0.25	0.22	0.20	0.18	0.17	0.16
250	3.72	0.70	0.47	0.35	0.28	0.24	0.21	0.19	0.17	0.16	0.15

Table E.6 χ_{LT} *for S460, Curve c,* $2 < h/b \leq 3.1$

$\lambda_z = L/i_z$	$\bar{\lambda}_z$	h/t_f									
		5	**10**	**15**	**20**	**25**	**30**	**35**	**40**	**45**	**50**
30	0.45	1.00	1.00	1.00	1.00	1.00	1.00	1.00	1.00	1.00	1.00
40	0.60	1.00	0.96	0.95	0.94	0.93	0.93	0.93	0.93	0.93	0.93
50	0.74	0.98	0.92	0.89	0.87	0.86	0.86	0.85	0.85	0.85	0.85
60	0.89	0.96	0.87	0.83	0.81	0.79	0.78	0.78	0.77	0.77	0.77
70	1.04	0.93	0.83	0.78	0.74	0.72	0.71	0.70	0.70	0.69	0.69
80	1.19	0.91	0.80	0.73	0.68	0.66	0.64	0.63	0.62	0.62	0.61
90	1.34	0.89	0.76	0.68	0.63	0.60	0.58	0.57	0.56	0.55	0.55
100	1.49	0.87	0.73	0.64	0.58	0.55	0.52	0.51	0.50	0.49	0.48
110	1.64	0.85	0.70	0.60	0.54	0.50	0.48	0.46	0.45	0.44	0.43
120	1.79	0.83	0.67	0.57	0.50	0.46	0.43	0.42	0.40	0.39	0.39
130	1.94	0.81	0.64	0.54	0.47	0.43	0.40	0.38	0.36	0.35	0.35
140	2.09	0.80	0.62	0.51	0.44	0.40	0.37	0.35	0.33	0.32	0.31
150	2.23	0.78	0.59	0.48	0.41	0.37	0.34	0.32	0.30	0.29	0.29
160	2.38	0.76	0.57	0.46	0.39	0.35	0.32	0.30	0.28	0.27	0.26
170	2.53	0.75	0.55	0.44	0.37	0.32	0.30	0.27	0.26	0.25	0.24
180	2.68	0.73	0.53	0.42	0.35	0.31	0.28	0.26	0.24	0.23	0.22
190	2.83	0.72	0.51	0.40	0.33	0.29	0.26	0.24	0.23	0.22	0.21
200	2.98	0.70	0.50	0.38	0.32	0.28	0.25	0.23	0.21	0.20	0.19
210	3.13	0.69	0.48	0.37	0.30	0.26	0.23	0.21	0.20	0.19	0.18
220	3.28	0.68	0.47	0.36	0.29	0.25	0.22	0.20	0.19	0.18	0.17
230	3.43	0.66	0.45	0.34	0.28	0.24	0.21	0.19	0.18	0.17	0.16
240	3.58	0.65	0.44	0.33	0.27	0.23	0.20	0.18	0.17	0.16	0.15
250	3.72	0.64	0.43	0.32	0.26	0.22	0.19	0.18	0.16	0.15	0.14

Example

533 × 210 × 122 UB

6 m between points of restraint, in S355 therefore curve c should be used (Table E4)

$h/b = 544.5/211.9 = 2.57$

$h/t_f = 544.5/21.3 = 25.6$

$L/i_z = 6000/46.7 = 128.5$

Taking $h/t_f = 25$

at $L/i_z = 120$, $\chi_{LT} = 0.54$

at $L/i_z = 130$, $\chi_{LT} = 0.51$

interpolating, at $L/i_z = 128$, $\chi_{LT} = 0.51$

$t_f = 21.7$, hence $f_y = 345$ N/mm^2

Then $M_{b,Rd} = \chi_{LT} W_y \dfrac{f_y}{\gamma_{M1}} = 0.51 \times 3200 \times 10^3 \times \dfrac{345}{1.0} \times 10^{-6} = 563$ kNm

APPENDIX F: EFFECTIVE LENGTH PARAMETER *k* AND DESTABILISING PARAMETER *D*

F.1 Effective length parameter for simply supported beams without intermediate restraint

The effective length parameter, k, for lateral torsional buckling of a simple beam with restraints at the ends may be conservatively taken as 1.0, or obtained from Table F.1. If restraint conditions at each end differ, the mean value of k should be taken.

For the destabilising load condition, the parameter D should be taken as 1.2, otherwise D should be taken as 1.0.

Table F.1 Effective length parameter, k

Conditions of restraint at supports		k
Compression flange laterally restrained.	Both flanges fully restrained against rotation on plan	0.7
Nominal torsional restraint against rotation about longitudinal axis	Compression flange fully restrained against rotation on plan	0.75
	Both flanges partially restrained against rotation on plan	0.8
	Compression flange partially restrained against rotation on plan	0.85
	Both flanges free to rotate on plan	1.0

F.2 Destabilising parameter *D*

In method 3, Section 6.3.2, the effect of destabilising loads may be taken into account by including a parameter D as follows:

$$\bar{\lambda}_{LT} = \frac{1}{\sqrt{C_1}} UVD\, \bar{\lambda}_z \sqrt{\beta_w}$$

For destabilising loads on simply supported beams, the parameter D should be taken as 1.2. (For non-destabilising loads D should be taken as 1.0.).

F.3 Cantilevers

F.3.1 Cantilevers with moment continuity, lateral and torsional restraint at the support

For this common case, the effective length parameter, k, and the parameter D should be taken from Table F.2, depending on the restraint condition at the cantilever tip.

F.3.2 Cantilevers without full lateral and torsional restraint at the support

The effective length parameter, k, and the parameter D should be taken from Table F.3.

If a bending moment is applied at its tip, the effective length parameter, k, should be increased by 30% or 0.3, whichever is the greater.

Table F.2 Effective length parameter k and destabilising parameter D for a cantilever without intermediate restraint, with effective restraint at the support

Restraint to Cantilever Tips	k	D
1. Free	1.0	2.5
2. Lateral restraint to top flange 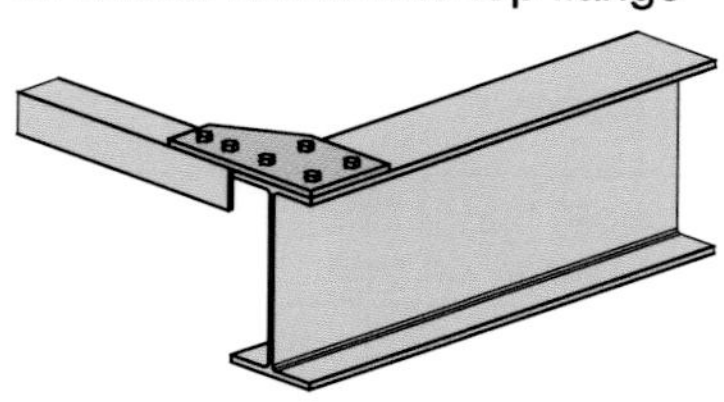	0.9	2.8
3. Torsional restraint 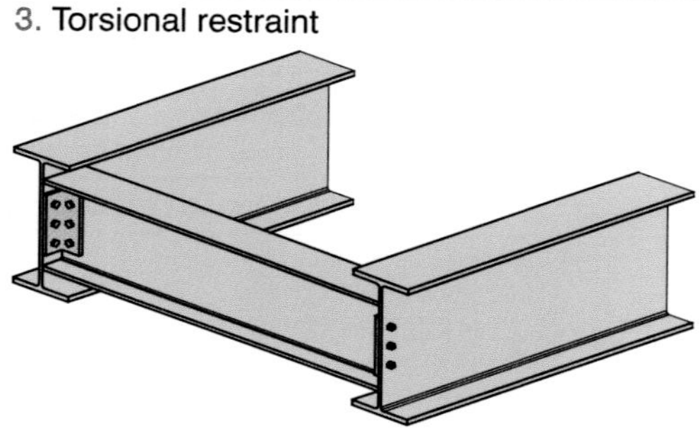	0.8	1.9
4. Lateral and torsional restraint 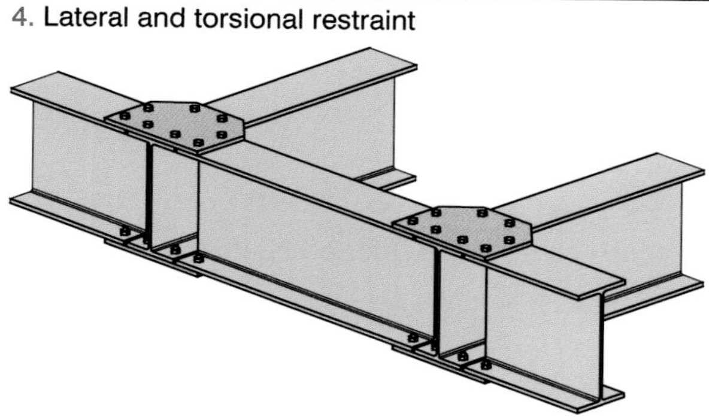	0.7	1.7

Examples of restraints to cantilever supports, all providing effective moment continuity and lateral and torsional restraint	
Cantilevered beam continuous over supporting beam, with lateral and torsional restraint	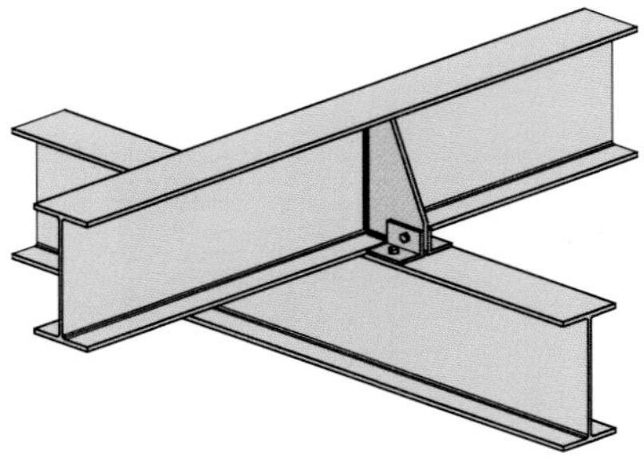
Discontinuous cantilever, at same level as continuous supporting beam	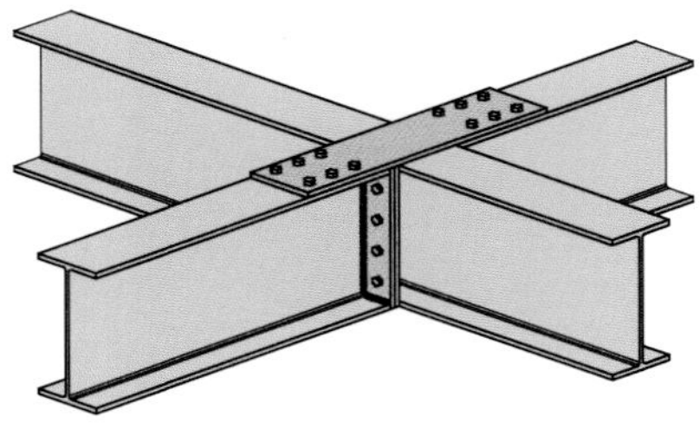
Cantilever supported from flange of column	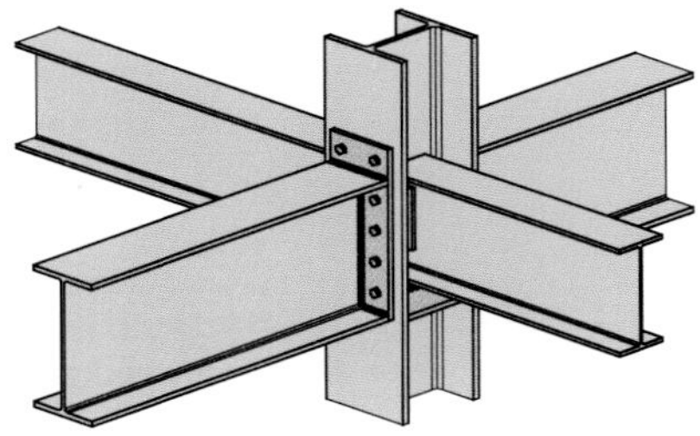

Table F.3 *Effective length parameter k and destabilising parameter D for cantilevers without intermediate restraint, for a range of restraints as the support*

Restraint Conditions		k	D
At Support	**At Tip**		
a. Continuous, with lateral restraint to top flange 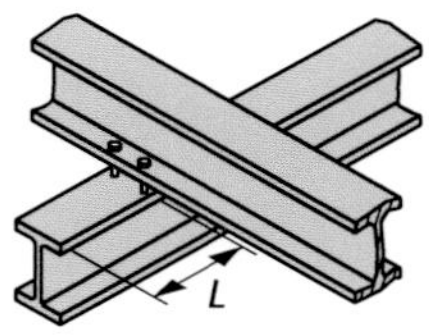	1. Free	3.0	2.5
	2. Lateral restraint to top flange	2.7	2.8
	3. Torsional restraint	2.4	1.9
	4. Lateral and torsional restraint	2.1	1.7
b. Continuous, with partial torsional restraint 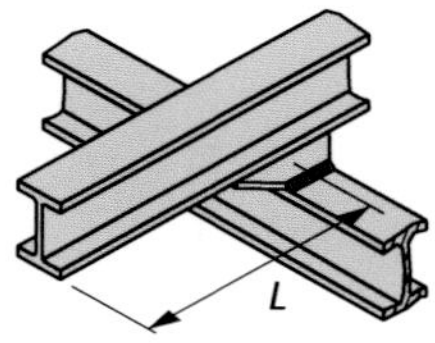	1. Free	2.0	2.5
	2. Lateral restraint to top flange	1.8	2.8
	3. Torsional restraint	1.6	1.9
	4. Lateral and torsional restraint	1.4	1.7
c. Continuous, with lateral and torsional restraint 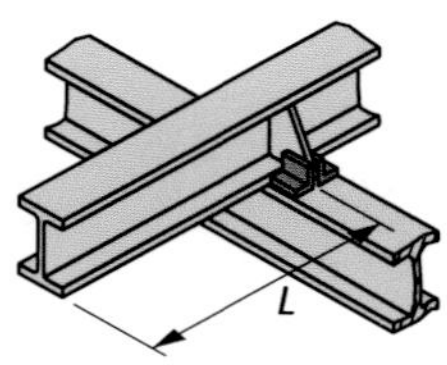	1. Free	1.0	2.5
	2. Lateral restraint to top flange	0.9	2.8
	3. Torsional restraint	0.8	1.9
	4. Lateral and torsional restraint	0.7	1.7
d. Restrained laterally, torsionally and against rotation on plan 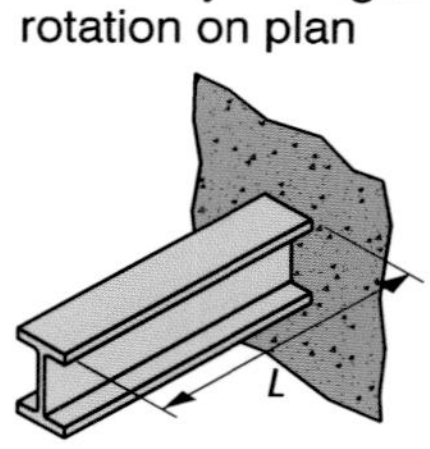	1. Free	0.8	1.75
	2. Lateral restraint to top flange	0.7	2.0
	3. Torsional restraint	0.6	1.0
	4. Lateral and torsional restraint	0.5	1.0

Tip Restraint Conditions

1. Free	2. Lateral restraint to top flange	3. Torsional restraint	4. Lateral torsional restraint
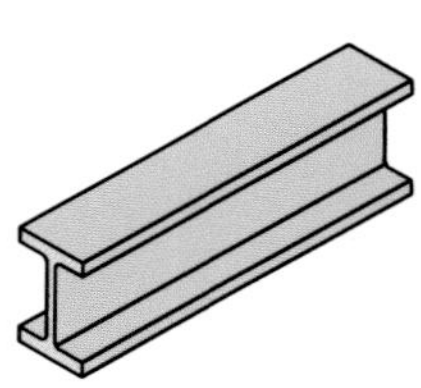	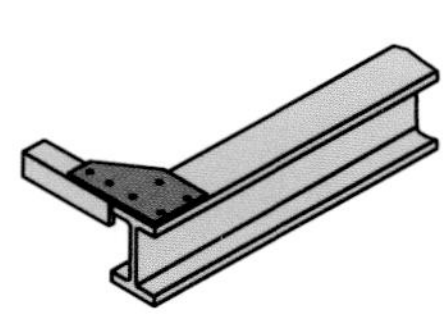	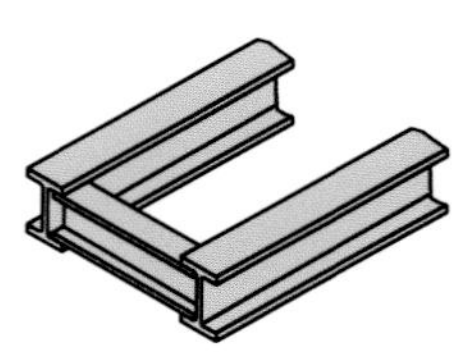	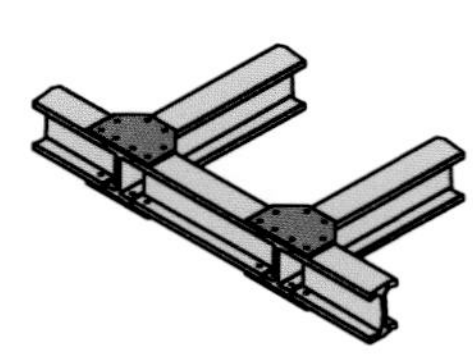
(not braced on plan)	(braced on plan in at least one bay)	(not braced on plan)	(braced on plan in at least one bay)